THE PATH OF
THE GREEN MAN

THE PATH OF THE GREEN MAN

Gay Men, Wicca, and Living a Magical Life

Michael Thomas Ford

CITADEL PRESS
Kensington Publishing Corp.
www.kensingtonbooks.com

CITADEL PRESS books are published by

Kensington Publishing Corp.
850 Third Avenue
New York, NY 10022

Copyright © 2005 Michael Thomas Ford

All Kensington titles, imprints, and distributed lines are available at special quantity discounts for bulk purchases for sales promotions, premiums, fund-raising, educational, or institutional use. Special book excerpts or customized printings can also be created to fit specific needs. For details, write or phone the office of the Kensington special sales manager: Kensington Publishing Corp., 850 Third Avenue, New York, NY 10022, attn: Special Sales Department; Phone: 1-800-221-2647.

CITADEL PRESS and the Citadel logo are Reg. U.S. Pat. & TM Off.

First printing: August 2005

10 9 8 7 6 5 4 3 2 1

Printed in the United States of America

Design by Leonard Telesca

Library of Congress Control Number: 2005922709

ISBN 0-8065-2653-X

FOR THE ORIGINAL GREEN MEN
MERRY MEET, AND MERRY PART, AND MERRY MEET AGAIN

Stars were falling deep in the darkness
as prayers rose softly, petals at dawn
And as I listened, your voice seemed so clear
so calmly you were calling your god

Somewhere the sun rose, o'er dunes in the desert
such was the stillness, I ne'er felt before
Was this the question, pulling, pulling, pulling you
in your heart, in your soul, did you find rest there?

Elsewhere a snowfall, the first in the winter
covered the ground as the bells filled the air
You in your robes sang, calling, calling, calling him
in your heart, in your soul, did you find peace there?

—"Full Circle" by Loreena McKennitt

Contents

THE PATH OF
THE GREEN MAN

Beginnings

Boston in winter is a bitterly cold place, the air so sharp that your breath clouds around your head with every exhalation and each footstep in the snow sounds like the rustling of a thousand frozen leaves. Walking through the city on a December night, it is easy to imagine the place in days gone by, the smoky waterside taverns crowded with sailors downing pints of ale and bowls of piping hot chowder to stave off the icy touch of the wind that whips down the cobblestone streets, chasing everyone indoors. It would be on such nights, around crackling fires, that tales would be told, songs sung, and laughter shared with friends. And it is this atmosphere that makes Boston the perfect place in which to celebrate the Pagan holiday of Yule, the longest night of the year when the world is cradled in darkness and those who still remember such things call back the light to plant the seed of life in the mouth of death.

The night of December 20, 1998, was not this kind of night. Although for weeks I'd hoped for a city that was wrapped in a glittering blanket of ice and snow and a sky stretching out over the rooftops in an unending ribbon of blackness speckled with the pale light of far-off stars, what I'd received instead was a day of unseasonably warm weather, bright sun, and all-around cheerfulness. These were not, I thought, ideal conditions under which to properly celebrate what was one of the most solemn of the old holidays.

Yet, that was exactly what I and nine other men were gathering that evening to do. Calling ourselves the Green Men, we were a group of gay men, all of whom in one way or another were interested in exploring Pagan spirituality. We'd discovered one another through various other connections, most of us through a drumming and chanting retreat held several months before. Others were friends, or friends of friends. We knew one another only vaguely, yet we had agreed to hold a ritual together and see what came of it.

As I sat in the darkened living room of the big, old house that was to be the stage for our ritual, I tried to get in the mood. It was difficult to imagine myself surrounded by the icy grip of winter when outside it felt more like the last lingering days of summer. At least, I consoled myself, the moon was cooperating. Only two days old, it hid its face from the world, sleeping soundly as it prepared to welcome the return of winter.

I was uncertain for other reasons as well. When I'd invited the other men to participate in a Yule ritual a month earlier, it had seemed like a great idea. But the truth was that I had no idea how the whole thing was going to come off. None of us did—most of us never having done anything even remotely like what we were about to undertake. We were a peculiar bunch with mixed backgrounds: a couple of lapsed Catholics, a convert to Hinduism, several agnostics, and a Radical Faerie. I myself was a former Baptist-Episcopalian-Buddhist. Only one of us had any real background in ritual and magic, and even that was minimal.

Primarily because the whole thing had been my idea, I was

the unofficial leader for the evening's activities. I had been thinking about the ritual for some time and was pretty well pleased with what I'd come up with. Still, sitting there moments away from beginning, it all seemed suddenly very ill prepared, very disorganized, very, well, silly. *Why*, I scolded myself, *didn't you just throw a holiday party.*

I pushed the thought from my mind and tried to focus on what we were there to do. I closed my eyes and thought about winter, of unending cold, blackness, and hunger. I thought, too, of how not only Boston but also the world was staring into the darkness. The day before I had written in my diary:

> The Wolf Moon has arrived with plenty of wildness. Today Bill Clinton was impeached in the House of Representatives, and the soon-to-be Speaker of the House, Rep. Bob Livingston, resigned before ever taking office, saying that an extramarital affair in his past disqualified him from being worthy of his position.
>
> Today also marked the fourth day of bomb attacks on Iraq for failing to cooperate with UN arms inspectors. And the 500th execution in America since the reinstatement of the death penalty in 1977 occurred in South Carolina yesterday evening when Andrew Lavern Smith was executed by lethal injection.

As originally celebrated by the farmers and the people of the land who kept the old traditions alive, Yule was a night of beseeching the sun to return and melt the icebound fields, to bring back the light that winter had stolen and hidden in the folds of its chilling cloak. Hundreds of years later, electric lights, imported produce, and central heating had made the situation slightly less dire, but still it seemed that we were longing for something to warm our souls, if not our skins and planting grounds. It was this thought I held in my mind as I waited to begin.

Befitting the season and our personalities, we had formed the circle for our ritual from a dozen yards of white tulle representing drifts of snow. An opening had been left on one side through which the participants could enter. The room was in total darkness. Myself and another man stood at either side of the circle's doorway as the others waited in the hallway.

At our call, each participant stepped forward and was smudged from head to foot with the smoke from a burning bundle of sage before entering the circle, a practice used by many spiritual traditions as a way of cleansing a person of negative energy. When everyone was inside the circle and seated, we then began the magical tradition of calling the directions, inviting the spirits of the North, East, South, and West to join us. Having nothing concrete to go on, those of us calling the directions simply made up our invocations as we went along.

The circle having been cast, I briefly explained what Yule was, why we were there to celebrate it, and why the Green Men had been created. Then I read a story I'd written for the occasion. Titled "The Gift of the Horned God," it was a mythlike story of one man who ventures into the green wood on the longest night of the year. There, he meets the Horned God, the ruler of the wild wood, and is given a spark of light to take back with him to help him through the cold of winter. He is also given a new name: the Green Man.

The story was meant as both a meditation on Yule and an introduction to what I saw as the purpose of the Green Men as a group. The Green Man himself represented not only each individual within the group but the very group itself. I asked the men to close their eyes as I read and to use the story as a guided meditation for their own journey into the darkness of Yule in search of the light.

I stopped at the point in the story where the Green Man comes across the Horned God sitting in his ritual clearing. The

Horned God is looking into his cauldron, which is filled with flames. He reaches into his cauldron and brings forth a gift. At this point, I asked the men to open their eyes. On doing so, they found me sitting before them dressed as the Horned God, wearing a mask I'd made from papier-mâché. There was a fire of lit rubbing alcohol (a nifty trick I'd learned from a Witch friend) burning in the cauldron before me.

The Horned God greeted the men and welcomed them to his glen. He asked them how their journeys were. Then he asked them to each name what he had come to his clearing in search of, and then to name what he had to give in exchange for receiving that desired blessing. We went around the circle, each man speaking until all had said their fill.

The Horned God then went around the circle giving each man a small quartz crystal, telling them to use it during the coming season of cold to meditate on the spark of light contained within them, a spark that would help them through the dark time. He then handed out green candles and had each man light his, saying, "See how as each one of us lights his candle the lights join to fill the room with brightness."

When all of the candles were lit, I removed my mask. A plate of homemade cookies and cups of water were passed around. The men then went around the circle again and discussed their experiences during the meditation. The reactions to the meditation were very encouraging. Different men saw different things when they encountered the Horned God in his glen— some their fathers, some lovers past or present, some a trusted friend. For most it was a very positive experience, and we talked a little bit about our expectations of the ritual and then what it was actually like for us. We then opened the circle and spent the remainder of the evening having dinner together and drumming.

Thinking back on that first ritual now, I still recall the feeling of joy that permeated the room when the ritual was over. All of us were excited, yet also filled with peace. My own feelings of happiness were mixed with ones of relief that everything had gone well. But most of all there was a sense of hope, a feeling that together we had created something that was going to come to mean a great deal to all of us. We had become the Green Men, and we had taken the first step on a journey that would lead us into a world of infinite possibilities. What would happen there, what adventures and challenges awaited us, we had no idea. But we knew we had begun something magical.

I cannot tell you what pattern of events led the others to the Green Men; I can speak only for myself. I had recently turned thirty, and possibly because of that many things in my life were changing. Among them was a renewed interest in spirituality. Raised Baptist, I had spent many years under the watchful eye of the Protestant God until, while attending an Evangelical Christian college, I had undertaken a minor rebellion and been confirmed in the Episcopal Church. With its long history, glorious cathedrals, and penchant for incense, wine, and ceremony, the Episcopal Church appealed to me much more than did the Baptist regimen of guilt, penance, and Communion provisions consisting of grape juice and small cubes of Wonder bread. Enchanted by the more cerebral aspects of Episcopal worship, I even applied to the seminary, lured there by visions of a lifetime spent in service to a God who favored music, poetry, and art above issuing commandments, throwing tantrums, and turning people into pillars of salt.

Seminary, however, was abandoned for a studio apartment in New York's Greenwich Village and a job as an editor at a large publishing house. Also discarded was my interest in the Christian God who had held such a prominent place in my life for the past twenty years. He was replaced by the teachings of the Buddha, a figure I had heretofore thought of only as a murky figure of interest to people who had not recognized the need to accept the saving grace of Jesus Christ. Once acquainted, I threw myself wholeheartedly into his teachings, attending weekly yoga classes and even regularly trekking uptown to a small, dusty apartment where a diamond cutter-*cum*-monk taught us elementary Sanskrit and the basic tenets of Buddhism. I shaved my head, stopped eating meat, and again considered the cloistered life.

Like my flirtation with Jesus, however, my relationship with the Buddha was not to last. Although meditation thrilled me and I found I could sit for hours in a full lotus position, there was something too ascetic about the practice for me. Oddly, it reminded me of my Baptist childhood, where pleasure was frowned on and thinking nice thoughts about one's enemies took priority over caring for oneself. I took away many excellent ideas from the books I read and the teachers I listened to, but deep inside I felt that my path lay elsewhere.

And so it was that, after moving from New York to the sleepy Boston neighborhood of Jamaica Plain, I found myself in a bookstore devoted to Pagan and Wiccan study (more on the differences between these two belief systems in chapter 1). It was not the first time. I had ventured into two such bookstores while living in New York. One had filled me with such a chilling sense of darkness that I had turned and left immediately; the other had been a hodgepodge of various alternative spiritualities, and as such had been less threatening but ultimately overwhelming in its multitude of choices.

Arsenic & Old Lace was different. A small, comfortable store, it was unapologetically devoted to Wicca and its related spiritual paths. On that first visit I think I purchased a candle and some incense, not sure where to begin but feeling that I had to buy *something*. On subsequent visits I acquired several books and, more important, developed a friendship with some of the staff. When an invitation to attend a monthly moon circle was extended, I accepted. Held in the store's basement, it was the first ritual I ever attended, and I immediately fell in love with the language, the ceremony, and, most important, the feeling it left me with as I walked home afterward.

During the next year I read extensively about Wicca and about the larger world of Pagan spirituality. I kept attending the moon circles, and I began doing my own daily meditations and rituals at home. I found in them the joy I'd found in the Episcopal services, but this joy was magnified a hundred times. Gone was the focus on guilt and the need for redemption, and in its place was a celebration of life and a belief that becoming a whole person didn't require forgiveness for imagined sins or denial of the pleasures of the world. This was not an abnegation of responsibility to others. Rather, it was a deeper acceptance of my place in the larger world, of my connection to the cycles of nature and my own role in them.

Yet, once again I found that something was missing, something that made my participation in the rituals I attended slightly bittersweet. And this time I knew what it was: Although I was always accepted as a gay man at the events I attended, gayness itself was never particularly celebrated as much as it was tolerated. Certainly the attitude toward gay and lesbian people was much more positive in the Pagan world than it had ever been in either the Christian or Buddhist communities, but still there was often a feeling of being the other, of not quite being part of the group.

Then, in October 1997, I received a flier about an event called the Twilight Covening. Organized by the EarthSpirit Community, a Wiccan group centered in western Massachusetts, this weekend retreat was devoted to Wiccan and Pagan practice. Participants signed up for one of a dozen or so "clans," groups devoted to a particular type of magical work. Although all of the clans sounded interesting, I ultimately chose the Eagle clan, which according to the brochure was ideal for those just beginning to study magic and ritual.

One of the two Eagle clan leaders was a very large, very wise, and very friendly gay man called Moose. For three days he led us through a series of basic magical rituals and meditations, introducing us to the core concepts of Wicca and helping us explore our own abilities and interests. Moose and I became instant friends, and after camp ended we continued a regular correspondence.

It was through these discussions with Moose that I decided to explore more deeply the appeal of Wicca to gay men. I collected books on many different aspects of Pagan spirituality in general and Wicca in particular, looking for references to gay men within these traditions. But time after time I came up empty-handed. Although several books discussed the "phenomenon" of all-female covens devoted to a practice of Wicca that excluded men and focused on the worship of the Goddess to the exclusion of a God, none discussed the inclusion of gay men within Wiccan traditions or explored how Pagan spiritual practices might specifically benefit gay men.

Finally, while reading the famed witch Sybil Leek's 1973 best-selling book *The Complete Art of Witchcraft*, I came across the following; "Most black magicians, real or alleged, are sexual perverts; this may account for the parallel rise in homosexuality and murders in California." Stunned by this ignorant statement, I almost put the book down. But Leek goes one step further, including in her book a chapter titled "The Place of the Homosexual in Witchcraft." Interested to see what she had to say, I read on. "Witchcraft," Leek writes in her book, "is a matriarchal religion acknowledging the Life Force as a link between all its associates. The homosexual, it would seem, could not entirely be concerned with witchcraft because of this basic belief in the Life Force." She then compares homosexuals to young people who seek spiritual freedom in too many drugs and too much sex. However, she graciously concludes that perhaps homosexuals *can* learn something from studying Witchcraft, but that they can never "rise to be part of the inner hierarchy of Wicca" because of their inability to work within the bounds of the male-female polarity Leek deems necessary for successful magical workings.

Given her age, background, and the times during which she wrote her book, one can almost—but not quite—forgive Leek for this idiocy. She was, after all, much better at theatrics than she was at writing. Still, it troubled me that a quarter-century after the publication of her book I still found gay people virtually excluded from discussions of Wiccan spirituality.

It was, I thought, time to change this. As my first step I located the local group of Radical Faeries, a nationwide network of queer men (and some women) who practice Pagan spirituality in a variety of forms. I attended a meeting and there met several wonderful men who, like myself, were intrigued by the idea of seeing just how Pagan spirituality and queerness could benefit from one another. Several months of meetings and discussions helped me shape my thoughts on the subject, and in the fall of 1998 the Green Men were born.

Since that time, and particularly after the publication of a series of pieces I wrote for the Radical Faerie–affiliated magazine *RFD*, many people have asked me to write about gay men and Wicca, to create a handbook of sorts that can be used by those interested in exploring Pagan spirituality and, specifically, how it relates to their lives as gay people. Certainly, there have already been books—and an increasing number of them—written about how gay men fit into spiritual traditions such as

Judaism, Christianity, Islam, and Buddhism, so why not about how we fit into Wicca and Paganism?

There have been a couple of books about gay men and Wicca, but not many. Perhaps this is because Wicca, by its very nature, is supposed to be inclusive of everyone. Perhaps because, unlike more established religious traditions, Wicca is not defined by any one set of beliefs, rules, or governing body subject to scrutiny and questioning. It is the most democratic of spiritual paths, a trait that makes it both one of the most joyously fulfilling and at the same time maddeningly frustrating to explore. Those seeking an introduction often find themselves overwhelmed by the available choices, and even those with more experience sometimes find themselves lost in a tangle of opposing ideas and options.

And so now I find myself putting my accumulated thoughts down on paper, detailing what I have come to see as the Path of the Green Man (or Green Man Wicca, if you like). My hope is that other men who, like myself, find themselves attracted to the possibilities of Wiccan and Pagan practice may find something here that helps them explore, define, and enjoy their own journey. My intention is to address both general questions— What is Wiccan and Pagan spirituality? What are the gods and goddesses? What is magic?—as well as topics of specific interest to gay men—How does my sexuality affect my practice? Are there gay gods and goddesses? How do I develop a personal spiritual system?

There are many aspects of Wiccan practice that are the same for everyone, gay and nongay. Then there are the aspects that are of specific interest to gay men. It would be impossible to write a useful, inclusive book for the latter group without discussing the general aspects of Pagan practice as well. Ultimately, this book is a primer for gay men interested in exploring Wiccan spirituality. You will find here general discussions of topics relating to Pagan spirituality as well as suggestions for meditation, rituals, and activities meant to further your connection to Wicca.

You will also find here an eight-part story cycle called "The Journey of the Green Man." These stories, beginning with the story I wrote for that first Yule gathering of the Green Men, follow the character of the Green Man through the eight major holidays, or sabbats, of the Pagan year (the Wheel of the Year, which is discussed in more detail in chapter 6). While some Pagans and Witches maintain very specific rituals and stories associated with the sabbats, the stories in this cycle draw from a number of sources. They are not a cycle unified by one common myth; rather, they are an example of how the different sabbats can be approached and what they might represent. Some of the stories are based on actual rituals done by the Green Men. Others are simply stories that may or may not suggest rituals the reader can do. The Green Man's journey mirrors the journey of someone exploring the Pagan world for the first time, and as such he represents all of us who undertake this journey. As you explore this book, you will become the Green Man, setting out on an adventure of self-discovery.

Where that adventure takes you is up to you.

Chapter 1

What We're Talking About

Witch. Magic. Pagan.

These words are simple ones, easy both to write and to speak. Beneath this simplicity of letter and sound, however, they are infinitely complex, capable of arousing both wonder and fear, joy and anger. Defining them is the work of a moment, yet understanding what they truly mean takes a lifetime and, some believe, many lifetimes.

Most of us are introduced to the figure of the witch as a Halloween bogey, a grizzled, crooked-nosed, black-caped figure streaking across the sky on her broom in search of toadstools and cobwebs with which to work her evil spells. Perhaps she takes the form of the cannibalistic sadist who fattens up Hansel for the cooking pot on a diet of gingerbread and candy, or maybe the green-faced Wicked Witch of the West who bedevils poor little Dorothy and her friends as they wend their way toward the Emerald City. However she appears, she is almost always ugly, almost always evil, almost always the enemy. When she is pushed into an oven or a house falls on her, we're supposed to applaud loudly, relieved to be rid of her.

I always sympathized with the witches in the fairy tales I loved so much as a child. The unnamed tormentor of Hansel and Gretel, for instance. Did she ask for her life to be upset by the sudden arrival of two whiny orphans? And Dorothy's nemesis, was she really not justified in seeking revenge for the death of her sister, especially after enduring the sanctimonious bubbliness of Glinda and her sickeningly sweet spun-sugar goodness? In general, the witches of legend are portrayed as bitter, jealous women bent on ruining things for anyone luckier, fairer, or more innocent than themselves.

If the witches of fairy tales have it bad, witches—alleged and otherwise—of the real world have had an even more difficult time of it. Time and again, the label of witch has been placed on those whose behavior, or merely whose appearance, has distressed those around them, often with fatal consequences. The infamous witch hunts of Europe resulted in the deaths of untold women and men. Although the exact numbers are a matter of often heated debate, we know that in some villages entire populations (mostly women, but also men) were executed for suspicion of dabbling in witchery, and ultimately the number of people who died at the hands of the witch-hunters is probably in the hundreds of thousands.

In America, the infamous Salem witch trials of 1692 resulted in far fewer deaths—twenty-four—but were no less disturbing, arising as they did largely out of a young woman's jealousy and escalating into all-out war between feuding neighbors, many of whom saw accusations of witchcraft as a convenient way to rid themselves of enemies.

Almost 300 years after the Salem tragedy, witchcraft once again became the focus of controversy in Massachusetts when, during the 1998 gubernatorial race, the Republican incumbent Paul Cellucci aired a television ad accusing his opponent, the Democratic state attorney general Paul Harshbarger, of defending the rights of witches. An immediate outcry came from the state's large and vocal Pagan community, and a lively protest at historic Fanueil Hall during a candidate debate found hundreds of witches chanting "Witches vote!" and waving signs of protest (mine said "I'M NOT A FANTASY, AND NEITHER IS MY VOTE").

Although no one was hanged or burned alive for speaking out about their beliefs at that rally, witches do still encounter discrimination due to prejudice and misunderstanding. Involvement in witchcraft has been used as the basis for denying child custody in cases of divorce, for firing people (particularly those in teaching or childcare positions), and even as "evidence" of guilt in trials. In some parts of the world—most notably in African nations—men and women are still tortured and killed after being accused of practicing witchcraft.

So what is a witch really? What are witchcraft and Wicca, how do they relate to Paganism, and what's with the whole capitalization issue (witch versus Witch and witchcraft versus Witchcraft) anyway? I'm a big believer in the power of language, and since understanding what these different words mean will help greatly in our discussions, and will help you as you explore your own connections to these worlds, we're going to have a little language lesson.

Paganism is the ground from which witches, Wicca, and witchcraft spring, so let's start there. The Latin word *paganus*, from which *pagan* comes, means "someone who dwells in the country." Similarly, the Old English word *hethen*, from which the later *heathen* is derived, simply means "someone who lives on a heath." Originally, neither word had religious overtones to it. Following the introduction of Christianity into European cultures, however, *heathen* and *pagan* became used to describe people who did not accept the notion of a spirituality centered around a single god figure.

It's interesting to see how these words evolved from simple

descriptives used to identify residents of the country to have much more derogatory connotations. Most dictionaries define a heathen as "a godless person," and *Merriam-Webster's Collegiate Dictionary*, eleventh edition, defines a Pagan as "one who has little or no religion and who delights in sensual pleasures and material goods."

Neither of these modern definitions is truly accurate. To understand what Paganism is, we need to return to the original Latin definition of someone who lives in the country. Before the advent of "organized" religion, spirituality most often centered around beliefs that arose out of experiences with and understanding of the natural world. At the most basic level, this kind of spirituality simply involved celebrating the cycles of nature. More developed forms of this belief system centered around deities, gods, and goddesses created to explain natural phenomena, such as the changing of the seasons, the eruptions of volcanoes, or the creation of the world.

Over time, and particularly because of the combined influences of increased scientific knowledge and the introduction of Christianity into European societies, the words *heathen* and *pagan* came to be applied to people who, either through geographic separation from centers of education or through refusal to accept either scientific findings or Christian teachings, continued to follow traditional beliefs. Today, the terms are generally meant to imply that a person does not follow a spiritual tradition centered around one single god, in particular the God (capital *G*) who stands at the center of Christianity, Judaism, and Islam.

Although failing to recognize this one-god concept is the primary definition of a Pagan, the underlying implication is that a Pagan is someone who is either too stupid to understand that only one god exists or else simply doesn't care and is more interested in pursuing sensual pleasures than in pursuing spiritual truth. Whichever way you look at it, this clearly is not a positive way of defining those who consider themselves Pagans.

What, then, is the truth? What is Paganism, and what makes someone a Pagan? The answers to these questions will, not surprisingly, depend on who you ask. A fundamentalist Christian's view of Paganism is going to be much different from mine, for example, because our belief systems differ. Even those who consider themselves Pagans are likely to disagree on the definition. For purposes of this book and our discussion, however, I am defining Paganism as a belief system centered around connecting with the cycles and processes of nature. A Pagan, therefore, is someone whose spirituality is rooted in connecting with the natural world and working to understand the connection we have to that world as human beings interacting with the rest of nature.

I know—this is as clear as mud, right? That's because, unfortunately, most definitions of Paganism focus on the rejection of a central god figure, as if that's the most important aspect of Paganism. The fact is, Pagan people may or may not incorporate the recognition of deity into their spirituality. But ultimately that's not the point. The point is that Paganism, whether it involves the worship of deities or not, is about exploring the cycles of nature and using what we learn from that exploration to improve both our lives and the state of the natural world.

Now, how does witchcraft and Wicca fit into all this? As I said earlier, Paganism forms the basis for witchcraft and Wicca. It's fairly safe to say—if not always true—that witches are almost always Pagans, but Pagans are not necessarily always witches. Then again, witches (lowercase *w*) are not always Witches (capital *W*), and witchcraft is not always Witchcraft or Wicca. Where Paganism is the recognition of the natural world, witchcraft may be seen as taking what is learned from observing the natural world and using that knowledge to effect change in your own life and in the world around you through various means such as ritual and magic (which we'll define a little later). In some sense, it's taking Paganism to another level.

I mentioned that not all witches are Pagans, although I would say most are. But there are witches who also consider themselves members of other religious traditions. For example, a friend of mine calls herself a Jewitch because she is deeply involved with both her local synagogue and a circle of witches who practice magic and ritual together. For witches such as this, the practices of magic and nature-centered ritual fit into their overall spiritual lives.

So what's the difference between witches and Witches, and Wicca and witchcraft and Witchcraft? Here's where it gets a little sticky. People tend to use all of these words to mean the same thing. But do they? As with so many things having to do with the Craft (a catch-all term for Wicca that many find much more useful than anything else), the matter is up for debate. Many see witches (lowercase *w*) as primarily people who practice the art of witchcraft (also lowercased) in the form of healing and magic using skills (e.g., herbs, divination, and what could be termed folk magic) without attaching any particularly formal spiritual associations to this work. These witches may be involved in other traditions and see their magical practices as simply part of an overall spirituality. On the other hand, Witches (capital *W*), may include along with their magical practices a more developed spirituality centered around a deity or deities associated with Pagan spirituality. For them, Witchcraft (capital *W*) is very much a focus of their lives, the primary guiding principle by which they live.

And what of Wicca? You will often see the terms *wicca* and *witchcraft* used interchangeably. Is there a difference? Again, that may depend on who you ask. From a language standpoint, *wicca* comes from the Old English word *wicca*, which was a masculine word meaning, basically, "a wizard." The feminine equivalent, *wicce*, meant "sorceress" or "witch." (By the way, a male witch is *not* a warlock, which is a derivation of the Middle English word *warloghe*, meaning "one who breaks an oath" and was used to describe untrustworthy people.)

The difference between Wicca and Witchcraft is, in my opinion, essentially a matter of esthetics and political correctness. Both are fully developed spiritual traditions having at their center Pagan principles. Wicca simply sounds less threatening and more legitimate than Witchcraft. "I'm Wiccan" or "I practice Wicca" is easier for some people to say or hear than "I'm a Witch" or "I practice Witchcraft." Books (including this one) are easier to sell if the word *wicca* is on the cover. Getting the U.S. government to officially recognize Witchcraft as a religion (which it did in 1986) was probably made easier by referring to it as Wicca.

But are there really any differences? Ultimately, not really. However, there are some people who would argue that Wicca is a more formalized way of practicing Witchcraft, particularly as outlined by Gerald Gardner (more on him in a bit). Just as there are variations on Christianity (Baptist, Catholic, Mormon, etc.) there are various forms of Witchcraft that have to do mostly with what deities are incorporated into practice and how the various rituals used in practice are carried out. Whether you call yourself Wiccan or Witch, however, is more a matter of personal preference than anything else. I will use the terms more or less interchangeably throughout the book, although personally I prefer Witch in general usage. Also, when referring to Witchcraft or Wicca as a belief system, or to Witches or Wiccans as part of that belief system, they will be capitalized. When referring to witches as a folkloric symbol or as characters, however, the word will be lowercased.

This brings us to one of the fundamental stumbling blocks

Witches encounter. One of the difficulties Witches have traditionally had with getting others to accept our religion is that people say that it's all made up, that it's not real because there's no one book (like the Bible), set of beliefs or rituals (like Mass), governing body or leader (like the pope), or even places of worship. This is true. In fact, the only real "law" of Witchcraft is what we call the Wiccan Rede, which says, "An it harm none, do as you will." In other words, if you're not hurting anyone, it's all good.

The message of the Rede isn't really that simple. Just as there are Muslims, Christians, and Jews who take the laws of their faiths and use them to justify all kinds of unpleasant activities, there are Witches who take the Rede as license to do whatever they want to. We'll discuss the issue of responsibility in more detail later, for now let's just say that if there's anything in Witchcraft that Witches follow as law, it's the Rede.

If there are none of the things you usually associate with a religion, then what makes Witchcraft a religion? Well, what makes Christianity or Judaism a religion? Any religion—whether it's practiced by billions of people all over the world or by one person in Des Moines, Iowa—is a set of beliefs that practitioners of the religion follow because they believe that doing so will improve their lives. Hindus believe that following the precepts of Hinduism will result in accumulation of good karma and, eventually, reincarnation into a more enlightened form. Christians believe that following the teachings of Jesus Christ will make them better people and, after their deaths, result in going to heaven.

It's important to remember that every religion, no matter what it is, was invented by human beings. Whether you believe that God spoke to Abraham and made a covenant with him or not, whether you believe that Jesus Christ was sacrificed for the sins of the world or not, whether you believe that Buddha or

Mohammed existed or not, whether you believe the teachings of these men are real and valid or not, the way in which these teachings are presented, and the way in which the faiths that have grown up around them are expressed, are all the work of human beings. It's human beings who created the rituals of Mass and baptism, human beings who drafted the bylaws and lists of things that must and must not be done to be a "good" member of a religious tradition.

There is a reason that religious traditions are called faiths. There is absolutely no scientific way to prove that anything promised by any religion is true. You simply have to have faith that it is. You cannot prove that there is a heaven, for instance, or that people who believe in the redemptive death of Christ go there when they die. There is no way to prove that we have souls, let alone that those souls are reborn again and again in different forms depending on our behavior. There is no way to prove the existence of angels, demons, or gods, miracles or divine punishments. These things, if we believe in them, have to be accepted purely on faith, simply because our personal experience leads us to believe that they are real, true, and valid.

What beliefs do Witches hold to be true? What deities and other beings do we believe influence our lives? Apart from the Rede, do we have anything concrete that we ascribe to? That depends on the Witch, and again, this is why it is so difficult for many people to perceive Witchcraft as a legitimate religion. But why is any religion valid? Simply because it's been around for thousands of years? Simply because there's a book at its center? Simply because entire cultures are devoted to it, wars fought over it, or trillions of dollars spent to keep it going?

The only thing that makes a religion valid is whether practicing it positively affects the life of the individual involved in it. If 7 million other people practice a religion, but following its beliefs doesn't work for you personally, then that religion isn't

valid for you personally. If twelve or thirteen people come together and engage in rituals and embrace beliefs that help them
lead more joyful, productive lives that affect the world for the
better, but you don't get anything out of what they do, it doesn't
make their religion any less valid.

One major thing that sets Wicca apart from other belief systems is that so many of the world's religions focus on what happens after death. Christianity looks ahead to the eventual war
between good and evil and the resulting eternity of peace,
where believers will live with God. Hinduism is centered around
being reborn into better circumstances. Buddhism is concerned
with recognizing that, essentially, nothing is ultimately of importance and that accepting this will (eventually) lead to en-
lightenment after a number of lifetimes.

Witchcraft is different. Although some (I would dare say
most) Witches do believe in reincarnation, the emphasis of
Wicca is not on death but on life. The rituals of Wicca are about
finding connections in the natural rhythms of the earth, and in
using those connections to manifest better lives for ourselves
and for everyone else we are connected to (which is, really, the
entire web of creation). Witchcraft is about experiencing
the world, not hiding from it, rejecting it, or waiting for something better to come along when we die.

I mentioned earlier that one of the dictionary definitions of
a Pagan is someone who delights in sensual pleasures. This is
true. Witchcraft encourages people to experience all of the
wonderful things the world has to offer, the incredible sights,
smells, tastes, and sounds. Eating, dancing, singing, laughing,
making love, making art—these are all ways of experiencing the
world around us. But experiencing them doesn't have to mean
abusing them. The implication of that dictionary definition is
that Pagan people spend all their time overindulging, where the
truth is that you can experience the world in ways that help you

appreciate it and lead you to making it better. That's what Wicca is about.

If Witchcraft has no leader or set of rules, then where did it come from? You'll occasionally hear people talk about Witch "families" or "lines." Supposedly, these are unbroken traditions of Wicca that have been handed down from one generation to the next. Do they really exist? It's an appealing idea, but probably not. The fact is, modern-day Wicca is cobbled together from all kinds of different traditions. The word *ancient* gets thrown around a lot when discussing Wicca, usually when someone wants you to believe that what he or she thinks or practices is valid. After all, it's difficult to argue against something with "ancient" origins, right? The truth is, although there certainly are some rituals, celebrations, and beliefs that have been around for thousands and thousands of years, with a few exceptions we have little evidence that any of these things were really part of any organized spiritual tradition, much less what we call Wicca today.

Most of what we practice in modern Witchcraft is stuff we've come up with based on bits and pieces of these "ancient" rites and beliefs. That's right: We made it up. Because there are so many traditional societies all over the world, Wicca has become a melting pot of sorts, with pieces of Native American ritual mixed with Celtic harvest festival practices, Egyptian beliefs mingled with Norse mythology. Unlike the world's major religions, which are more or less unified by the teachings of a single spokesperson, Pagan beliefs differed from country to country, and often from village to village. Coming up with one single view to base Wicca on would be impossible, and so what we have is a spicy stew in which the best of the world's many different Pagan traditions have been combined.

There have, not surprisingly, been attempts to organize Witchcraft into a more unified system. Most notably, Gerald

Gardner, a British Witch, set down an organized system of ritual (now known as Gardnerian Wicca) and wrote several influential books, in particular *Witchcraft Today*, that had an enormous effect on both generating interest in Witchcraft and in creating the problems associated with defining what Witchcraft is and isn't. Considered by many to be the founder of modern-day Wicca, Gardner himself refuted the idea that he had "invented" Wicca and claimed to be an initiate into a long-standing coven. Like so much of Wicca's "history," Gardner's claims cannot be documented, and as such are a matter of personal speculation.

Ultimately, it doesn't matter whether Gardner was truly passing along information and traditions that were hundreds or thousands of years old or if, as is more likely, he simply assembled some lovely rituals and ideas drawn from a multitude of sources. The point is, what he created resonated with a lot of people, and Witchcraft became very popular in a very short time thanks to Gardner and to students of his such as Sybil Leek and Raymond Buckland, who themselves brought many of Gardner's ideas to the United States.

What was this religion that Gardner and others set forth? Essentially, Wicca as a nature-based religion built around the conjoined concepts of worshiping a central Goddess figure and working magic. The Goddess can take many forms and have many names, but basically she embodies the Divine Feminine in nature. A God also exists, but his role is principally that of a consort to the Goddess rather than the patriarchal figure who features so heavily in most of the world's religions. In Gardnerian Wicca, rituals and magic are performed by a group, or coven, of Witches and are designed both to celebrate the Goddess in her many forms and to effect change through the application of energy into magical work (more on this in chapter 6). Although male members of the coven act as priests, it is the women who occupy the most important roles in leading the group. And by the way, the whole notion of a coven consisting of thirteen members is not necessarily true. Covens may have any number of members, and a group of Witches may call themselves a coven, a circle, the Monthly Full Mooners, or anything else they like.

Although Wicca as it was initially introduced into America of the 1950s had wide appeal, there was one fundamental flaw with Gardner's teachings: they were based entirely on a heterosexual model. His rituals and underlying theories centered around a primary Goddess figure, and the magical workings of Gardnerian circles largely involved Witches working together in male-female pairs, which Gardner considered necessary for successful magical work due to the opposing and complementary energies contained within men and women.

We'll go into more detail about this concept, and its effect on gay men in the world of Witchcraft, in chapter 2. How Gardner and adherents such as Leek (whose ridiculous comments about gay people and Wicca were discussed earlier) came up with these notions is something only they know. The truth is, they, like most of the world at that time, probably simply had no experience with gay people and didn't think much about them. Also, there is probably more than a little truth to the accusation that a good deal of the initial interest in Wicca came from men who were interested in seeing a lot of naked women and thought this was a great way to get ladies to take their clothes off.

Elevating the Goddess to the principal role of a religion was a novel idea, particularly in the 1950s and 1960s. In addition, the counterculture that was beginning to rebel against the straight-laced establishment embraced anything new, particularly if it upset the status quo. For all of these reasons, Witchcraft flourished, and as it did, various people wanted to put their imprint on it. Soon, Gardnerian Wicca was just one of many forms, and it wasn't long before what "real" Witchcraft was became a question no one could really answer.

Things became even more interesting in the United States in the late 1970s with the publication of Starhawk's seminal book *The Spiral Dance*. Probably even more than Gardner's work, this book introduced the concept of Witchcraft to a whole new audience. Starhawk, however, referred to this exciting spiritual path as the "ancient religion of the Goddess." Although her book contained many concepts and rituals familiar to those who had experience with Witchcraft, this new and improved version was somehow easier to digest. The underlying notion was that a long-standing tradition of feminine deity worship had been reclaimed (an entire movement called the Reclaiming Tradition would eventually be the direct result of the book's publication), an idea that spoke strongly to people, especially women, who were fed up with traditional, male-dominated spirituality.

The importance of *The Spiral Dance* cannot be overemphasized. Starhawk, herself coming from a Jewish background, presented people with a coherent, accessible, and empowering means of expressing themselves in a way that was new and exciting. And unlike Gardner, she was very careful to stress that spirituality went hand in hand with politics, a message that rang loud and clear in an era where politics of all kinds were front and center in the American consciousness. This, perhaps, is her greatest contribution to the world of Witchcraft. Where before one's involvement in Wicca was generally seen as a secret thing, Starhawk encouraged truly living the principles of Witchcraft and using them to manifest real changes not just in oneself, but in the world at large. Participation in demonstrations against political oppression and environmental destruction, fighting for human rights and economic justice, and striving to be politically aware and active were, and still are, hallmarks of those who follow the Reclaiming Tradition.

Starhawk's vision of Witchcraft also differed from Gardner's in that it moved away from the male-female notions of energy and focused instead on using an individual's distinctive qualities to effect change, regardless of gender. For those of us who did not fit neatly into the traditional male-female polarity model, this was groundbreaking stuff. I can still vividly recall discovering the book in 1988 while taking the first-ever women's studies class offered at the fundamentalist Christian college I attended. Already a center of controversy among both the student body and the faculty, the class drew even more attention when word got out that the instructor was promoting Witchcraft, despite the fact that all she had done was include the title of Starhawk's book in a bibliography of books about women's spirituality.

I badly wanted to read the book, but I had no idea where to find it, Amazon.com and the like not yet being available. Finally, I tracked it down at a dingy, strange-smelling, and decidedly shady bookstore devoted to occult topics. Time and again I picked it up and put it down, afraid to open it. Eventually, I left the store empty-handed, the threat of heresy hanging over my head like a raincloud. It would be another ten years (and twenty years after the book's original publication) before I would actually buy *The Spiral Dance* and read it. That same year I would attend one of Reclaiming's famous "Witch Camps," where I would meet Starhawk herself and, later, interview her for my book *Paths of Faith*.

Although Starhawk and her book are the road by which many women and men—straight and gay—came to Witchcraft, no such door was opened specifically for gay men. Lesbians in some ways fit naturally into the Goddess-focused world of Witchcraft, and many did embrace it wholeheartedly, either as parts of mixed-gender groups or in all-women groups. Gay men, though, were left to take what they could find, and with a few exceptions along the way, this is how things have remained. In the next chapter we'll talk about how and why Wicca can be such a powerful spiritual path for gay men, and why I think gay men deserve their own tradition.

Because of its fluid nature, Witchcraft appeals to a wide range of people. Some of these people are dissatisfied with the religious traditions they were brought up in, while others want to find additional ways of exploring their spiritual sides. Wicca often provides a safe, encouraging atmosphere for people to express themselves in ways they don't feel comfortable doing elsewhere. Frankly, this open environment can sometimes make Witchcraft seem like a free-for-all. If you attend virtually any Pagan event, you're bound to encounter all kinds of people, from those who wouldn't seem out of place in a business office to those who express their spirituality by dressing up in costume and insisting that everyone call them "Moonglow Snakedancer" or "Thistledown Bunnyman."

This sometimes circus-like atmosphere that can surround Pagan and Wiccan events doesn't help as far as the serious factor goes. But it's part of what makes Witchcraft so much fun to be involved with. This isn't to say that Wicca doesn't have its share of less-than-balanced individuals hanging around. Every religion does. It's just that, when it comes to Wicca, these personalities are often much more recognizable than, say, the Mormon elder who secretly smokes and drinks or the Baptist minister who spends his midnight hours in S&M chat rooms. People are attracted to religion for all kinds of reasons, not the least of which is that they think it will cure all of their emotional issues.

Despite all the strikes against it as far as being the new kid on the religious block, Wicca is indeed an official religion as far as its legal status. Not that having a government consider you valid makes you valid, but it's nice that Wicca is afforded legal protection. Ironically, this is due in large part to the U.S. military and prison system. After legal challenges were brought by Wiccans demanding equal opportunities to practice their religion in the armed forces, the U.S. government was forced to recognize Witchcraft as a spiritual tradition as valid as Judaism, Islam, and Christianity.

This doesn't mean things are easy for Wiccans in these places. Although Witches do currently serve in the armed forces and conduct rituals on military bases, and although Wiccans are permitted to practice in U.S. jails, prejudice still remains. Even within the Wiccan "community," differences of opinion over what's right and true have led to some ugly confrontations and long-standing feuds (a situation not unfamiliar to anyone who has ever experienced the similarly fractious gay "community").

A quick glance through any Witchcraft-oriented Web site, book, or message board will yield numerous examples of this kind of infighting and posing. You can only be a Witch if you're part of a coven, one site will admonish, while another posts information for the solitary practitioner. You must be initiated into Wicca by another Witch, says one source, only to be contradicted by the book offering a beautiful and moving self-initiation ritual. You can only be a real Witch if you're Irish. You have to worship only the Goddess. You need to procure a three-foot silver dagger and rinse yourself in saltwater collected in a seashell under a full moon or you have no business calling yourself a Wiccan.

Bullshit. Again, I cannot stress enough that although Witchcraft is a very serious spiritual path with deeply important and life-changing ideas at its core, everything else is ornamentation. Anyone who tells you that you have to do something a certain way, believe in a particular deity, or use exact language is com-

pletely and utterly wrong. There are no deep, dark secrets that
need to be passed down to you in forest clearings by coven
members dressed in robes. There are no mystical incantations
that, when uttered on the night of the new moon, will make
you suddenly wise and powerful.

The viability of Witchcraft, like that of all religions, is measured by how much practicing it changes your life for the better. People who demand that you believe what they believe or
do what they do are simply insecure about their own paths.
They're searching to legitimize their practice by making yours
look inadequate, and they are not to be believed or trusted. If
you meet a teacher—any teacher—who says that her or his way
is the only right way, that person is a liar. If you encounter
someone who judges your practice and says your faith isn't
valid, ask yourself what motivates that person to think that way.
Ultimately, only you really know how your spiritual path is or is
not working for you.

With so many different permutations of Witchcraft existing
today, how do you know which one is right for you? Partly, you
discover this by educating yourself. That means reading as
much as you can about Wicca and sifting through the nonsense
(and there's a *lot* of nonsense out there masquerading as useful
fact) to get to the heart of things. But reading will only get you
so far. The real way to find out what form of Witchcraft—or if
any form of Witchcraft—works for you is to experience it for
yourself.

Each chapter in this book contains an exercise or exercises
designed to help you begin exploring Wicca, and chapters 7 and
8 go into more detail about creating a magical community
and living a life centered in Wiccan practice. For right now,
though, I encourage you to explore the world of Paganism and
Witchcraft by reading what others have said about it. I come to
this topic with my own ideas and prejudices, just as anyone dis-

cussing their spiritual path does, and I certainly don't assume that what works for me will work for everyone. At the end of the book I list a number of other books that I feel present a fairly wide-ranging look at how Witchcraft is practiced by different kinds of people. This is by no means a comprehensive list, but it is a starting point for your exploration of Wicca.

THE GIFT OF THE HORNED GOD
A Story for Yule

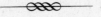

ABOUT YULE

Yule, or the winter solstice, is the first sabbat (major celebration) of the Pagan year. It is the longest night of the year, and while it is considered one of the Lesser Sabbats, it is for me one of the most enchanting.

The word *Yule* comes from the Norse *iul*, meaning "wheel," a particularly fitting name for the first stop on the cycle we know as the Wheel of the Year. Because the winter solstice marks the longest night of the year, Pagans saw it (and continue to observe it) as the night on which the sun died and, at dawn on the following morning, was reborn, or at least renewed his promise to return. The appearance of the sun after the cold, dark night was a sign that spring would return, even if it would take some time.

It doesn't take much effort to see how this Pagan festival was Christianized to make it acceptable to the church. Christ takes over the role of the sun, while his mother, Mary, assumes the Goddess role. More distressing, at least to me, is the commercialization of the holiday. Yet, the original power of Yule can still be felt in many of the traditional carols, and even good old Santa retains some of the Pagan about him, resembling as he does a magical figure who arrives to bestow blessings on those who believe in him.

This Yule story is based on the concept of initiation. It seemed fitting to me that the Green Man should begin his journey by meeting the Lord of the Green Wood, the Horned God who is the focus of Green Man spirituality and who symbolizes many things, including nature, sex, mystery, manhood, wisdom, wild magic, and joy. It is the Horned God who calls many of us to the path in the first place, and so I wanted him to send us on our way with a blessing and a challenge.

THE TIME OF GREAT cold had come. For weeks the sun had retreated more and more into itself, leaving behind only shadows and darkness. Then the snows had swept down on the land, covering all with a thin blanket that froze the Earth and lulled her to a sleep from which no amount of shaking or calling would wake her.

Now it was the birthday of winter, and the man shivered in his house where the hearth lay cold and the windows cracked with frost. As the wind spirits danced around the walls and taunted him by calling down the chimney and blowing out the fire, he thought bitterly of the warmth of summer. He longed to sing, but the words had turned to ice in his throat, and he could remember none of the tunes. In silence, he rubbed his numb hands together and recalled the caress of the sun on his skin.

And so it was that on the longest night of the year the man stepped out into the mouth of the darkness and went in search of the sun. Wrapped only in his tattered cloak, he struggled against the breath of the frost giants, climbing along the broken path into the mountains as they did their best to blow him back down into the valley. But his heart was fierce, and he bent his head to the giants' roars and put one foot in front of the other.

He climbed for most of the night, and as the moon rose pale

as bone over the top of the mountain, the man found himself at an unfamiliar pass. The winds whipped his cloak from his shoulders, and his skin burned with cold. Seeing him near defeat, the frost giants clapped their great hands and sent a blizzard to claim him.

Surrounded by the swirling snow, the man put his hands before his face and tried to find his way. He turned first to one side and then another. But all about him the whiteness turned in great sweeping circles, blinding his eyes. He knew neither up nor down, left nor right, and he felt his heart beginning to freeze in his chest. He could go no farther, and suddenly he wanted nothing more than to sleep, to dream the cold dreams of winter. The snow welcomed him into its arms, and he heard its sweet lullaby in his ears.

But just as he was about to surrender, he saw through the blizzard a flash of light. It came from a crack in the mountain, appearing in a brief moment when the wind parted the curtains of ice. The man saw it, and his heart propelled him forward with his last breath. He found the crack, placed his foot inside it, and then knew no more.

When he awoke, he was bathed in thin light. He looked about him and saw that he was at the entrance to a forest. Behind him was the crack through which he had passed, and beyond it the storm continued to rage. But inside the mountain it was early summer. The grass around him was green and long, and the flowers gave off the scent of growing things.

The man stood up, testing his legs. The cold had lessened, and he was able to walk more easily. And so he entered into the forest, passing beneath the entwined arms of two large oak trees and into the green light of leaves. The sounds of birds called him forward, and soon he found himself walking quickly along the path, following it as it twisted and turned through the strange forest, taking him ever deeper into the mountain.

After a time, he noticed that he was not alone in the woods. He caught glimpses in the trees of hares and foxes, their eyes shining brightly in the summer light as they darted here and there in the ferns. And the deep dark eyes of stags sometimes met his for a moment before they blinked closed and disappeared with a gentle rustling of leaves. The sight of them filled him with laughter, and he walked faster.

The path began to go up, and still he followed it. He found himself following a stream of clear water, which came to an end at a deep pool into which a waterfall tumbled from a great height. In the depths of the pool the man saw the rainbowed bellies of salmon flashing. He looked up to the place where the waterfall fell from a mossy mouth and he began to climb.

The climb was hard, but whenever he felt close to giving up he discovered a rock on which to pull himself up, or a foothold in which to place his boot. In this way, he climbed the waterfall and came to the top.

There, he found a clearing. A circle of thirteen trees grew close to each other, forming a grove. In the space made by their leafy crowns the sky opened blue and sweet, and at their feet the land was green.

Sitting beneath the largest of the trees was the Horned God. His hands rested gently in his lap and his eyes were closed. Around him were the animals of the forest, the foxes, hares, and stags who had followed the man on his journey. When they saw him, they whispered to one another, and the Horned God opened his eyes.

"So, you have come," he said to the man. His voice was as warm as the breeze that rippled the leaves in summer and as gentle as the rain that sang to the man as it fell on his roof at night.

"I have come in search of the sun," the man said. "The world is asleep and she will not wake."

The Horned One looked at the man for a long time. Then

he spoke again. "What will you give me in exchange for the sun?" he asked.

The man had no answer. He had nothing worthy of giving to the Lord of the Green Wood.

"You have everything already," he said helplessly. "The whole of the wood is yours. The beasts do your bidding. You know the secrets of life and death."

The Horned God turned his gentle eyes on the man, and in them he saw both fierceness and joy. "I will give you the sun," he said, "but I demand a price. I demand a song."

"A song?" said the man. "But what is that to you? Surely all the songs of the birds are already yours."

"Sing to me of the sun," said the Horned One. "Sing to me of summer and love and magic and what they mean to you. Sing to me of what is in your heart. Sing to me of these things, and I will give you what you ask."

The man closed his eyes. He stilled his thoughts and let his mind fill with the voice of his heart. Then he opened his mouth and sang. He sang of love, magic, joy, birth, and creation. He barely heard the words as they tumbled from his throat and filled the grove, but he knew that they spoke of his deepest desires. They told of what he had lost and wanted to find once more.

When he was done, he opened his eyes and saw that a cauldron was sitting before the Horned God. Bright, clear fire jumped in its depths, illuminating the face of the Lord of the Green Wood. The man waited anxiously for him to speak.

"You see," said the Horned One. "You gave me something I did not have. You gave to me the only thing that you have that is truly your own. You gave me your story. And for that I will give you in return two things. First I will give you your name. From this time on you shall be called Green Man, for you love all that grows wild and free. But with this name comes a great debt, for it ties you forever to the Earth and to her cycles of birth and death, change and renewal. It asks that you embrace her in her coldness as well as in her warmth as you travel with her the path she takes throughout the year. Are you willing to do these things?"

The man looked into the eyes of the Horned God and spoke. "Yes," he said. "I am willing to do these things." And he knew that he spoke the truth.

"Then I will give you my second gift," said the Lord of the Green Wood. "I will give you the sun."

The Horned God reached into the cauldron. Then he drew out his hand and opened it. Sitting in his palm was a small clear stone.

"But that is not the sun," said the Green Man. "It is as cold and lifeless as a piece of ice."

"Take it," said the Horned One, "and look into its depths."

The Green Man took the stone and held it in his hand. He looked into it; deep within its center he saw a spark of light.

"Just as the frozen Earth holds within it the seeds of spring, the stone holds within it the light you long for," said the Horned God. "Take it back to the world of cold and winter. Hold it in your hand and know that you hold the seed of light. Plant it in your heart. Sing to it, as you did to me. And in time, it will grow into the sun. When it is too big for your heart to contain, it will begin to fill up the sky. And when it has grown large enough, it will call back summer from her resting place in the Earth to throw it like a ball into the air."

The Green Man placed the stone inside his shirt, close to his heart, where he felt it warming him.

"Now go," said the Horned One. "Turn and dive from this place into the pool at the bottom. You will not be hurt. And when you emerge, remember the seed you carry with you. And remember, too, your name."

The Green Man turned and walked through the opening in the circle of trees where the land gave way to empty space. Far below him he saw the pool, and the salmon turning in the waters. His heart trembled.

"Do not be afraid," said the voice of the God behind him. "It is all my world, and you are safe within it."

The Green Man took a deep breath, filling his chest with air. Then he dove out into the warm sky. He felt himself tumbling down, rushing toward the water and rocks beneath it. But as he fell, he was filled with joy.

The water closed around him, and as it rushed past his body he saw the glint of gold and silver as the salmon scattered. He waited to feel the bottom beneath his fingers, but he kept going down, farther and farther until he was sure the air in his chest would take him no deeper.

Then he was through. In a moment the water changed to cold air, and he saw that it was night and he was lying once more in drifts of snow. He stumbled to his feet and turned every which way, but there was no sign of the crack he had passed through into the mountain, no sign of the green wood or the pool. He was standing again in the pass, with the storm raging about him furiously.

At first he was overcome with grief and rage. It had all been a trick played on him by the frost giants. But then he felt the cloak that was wrapped around him. It was not his old one, but one of strong wool the color of the deep forest. Then he remembered his name, and who he was. Quickly, and with trembling hands, he reached inside and felt in the pocket at his breast. There he found the stone given to him by the Horned God. He held it for a moment, feeling the light within it touch his fingers.

The Green Man found the path that led out of the mountains and took it. Again, the snow beat at him and the cold tried to claim him for its own. But now the Green Man's heart was light. His footsteps were sure, and the song that flowed from his throat was one of light and coming warmth.

When he arrived home, the Green Man took the stone from its hiding place. He lit a candle, and it seemed to him that the light it cast was brighter than any he had ever seen. He then built a fire. This time, the winds did not come down the chimney to blow it out, and soon his home was filled with its merry warmth.

As the Green Man sat before the fire, thinking of the Horned God and his gift, he held the stone in his hand and listened to the winter storming around his house. He knew that it would remain for some time to come. But now he welcomed the darkness as a time of rest and contemplation, of preparing for the next season. He knew that within the blackness and the cold the seed of light would grow. He would sing to it and tell it his stories. One day, when it was stronger, it would find its place in the sky. And in helping it grow, so would he grow, until the time came for him to once more visit the grove of the Horned God and share with him what he had learned from the journey begun on this longest of nights.

Chapter 2

Wicca and Gay Men

In chapter 1, we talked a little bit about the history of Wicca in the United States, beginning with the introduction of Gerald Gardner's teachings in the 1950s and looking at the evolution these ideas underwent, resulting in movements such as the Starhawk-inspired Reclaiming Tradition. Certainly, there are many other manifestations of Witchcraft, each with its own unique qualities, theology, and ways of doing things. One of the best things about Wicca is its ability to include people of all types.

In discussing the different views of Wicca that exist, I cannot stress the importance of remembering that no one owns Witchcraft. There is no central authority. There is no one who can claim to have all the answers or to know how everything should be done. The different rituals that exist, the beliefs that are espoused, and the theories that are set forth all come from the minds of human beings who invented them based on their experiences. With the exception of a few basic underlying principles that we'll discuss shortly, Wicca can be adapted to work for anyone who is willing to devote time and energy to exploring its possibilities.

In an ideal world, this should be true of any religion. Religions, as we've previously discussed, are simply sets of instructions people follow to make their lives better. As we all know, this ideal has been distorted time and again by people more interested in gaining power and control than in truly developing a spiritual path. Wicca is no exception. There are people involved in Witchcraft whose sole purpose seems to be to accumulate followers, adoration, and money. There are people involved in Witchcraft who are just plain nuts. There are people involved in Witchcraft who claim to be the one true voice. All of these people do a deep disservice to the Craft because they prevent others from really understanding what it's all about.

Gay men, in particular, I think have been at a disadvantage in the Wiccan community. Understanding why first involves a more thorough discussion of some of the theories behind Wicca. As you know, the basis of Witchcraft is nature. More precisely, Witchcraft encourages us to really look at the cycles of nature and see how we fit into them. This means looking at and experiencing both the "good" and the "bad." We should more properly say the light and the dark, although these words, too, have connotations that obscure what we're really talking about.

For everything that exists there is an opposite. There is light and dark, yin and yang, life and death. Too often, we assume that one-half of these pairs is good and the other half is bad, which isn't true. Yin and yang are a more accurate set of opposites, representing not opposing forces but complementary ones, neither truly whole without the presence of the other. So it is with nature's cycles. All living creatures are born, live for a span, and die. Day follows night. Summer turns to fall. Without one, the other would not be the same. Yet, too often we focus only on one aspect to the exclusion of the other.

Witchcraft teaches us to fully explore both sides of a pair. Frequently, even Witches forget this, concentrating only on what they see as good, light, and happy and pushing aside the opposites. But when these other areas of nature—of life—are explored as well, then a full picture of what it means to be part of the ever-turning cycles of nature emerges.

We'll talk about how this works in more depth later on. The point is, almost everything we do in Wicca is based on this concept of complementary energies. Because of this, teachers such as Gardner believed that in order for a Wiccan circle to be successful, it must be comprised of male-female pairs. Obviously, the notion derives from the idea that men and women possess different kinds of energy that, when put together, create something powerful. It also is a physical manifestation of the Wiccan reverence for the Goddess and the idea that her male consort is there to worship and support her.

Although I respect this idea and do believe that for many Witches it may be true that working with someone of the opposite gender is a powerful experience, I also think we have to totally rethink the notion of gender and its purpose when it comes to Wicca. I reject completely the assertion made by a number of Witches that only women, for example, can fully understand the power of Wicca or fully connect with the Goddess. This is, frankly, as stupid as the Catholic Church's teaching that only men can fully connect with God and therefore women cannot be priests.

No one owns the divine. No one is better equipped because of gender to connect with the divine. Again, these kinds of notions are perpetuated by people who want to feel important, who want to corner the market on spirituality for themselves and let in only those they think are worthy. In my opinion, these people are not true proponents of spirituality, but rather hindrances to the expression of truth.

Now, this is not at all to say that gender-oriented work cannot be powerful. It can. In fact, Green Man spirituality is based on groups composed solely of gay men. And there are numerous all-women covens, for example, where the participants feel their spiritual work is enhanced by the single-sex makeup of the group. I'm not saying that male-female working groups don't have validity or that single-gender groups are somehow superior. What I am saying is that we need to look at *why* different types of groups work.

I think those who push the necessity of male-female polarity are missing the point. I don't believe that such pairings work because men and women have inherently different energies that need to be brought together. I think they work because the people involved are most comfortable working with one another and because the energy of the *individuals*—regardless of gender—complement one another.

All of us, simply by virtue of being human, have varying personalities, gifts, and outlooks. All of this can be grouped together as our personal "energy." If you think about the people in your life, it's easy to pinpoint what kind of energy different people have: depressing, uplifting, positive, negative, aggressive, and passive. Sometimes these different types of energy may apply more frequently to people of a certain gender, but most of the time they're fairly equally divided among the sexes.

Gay men have frequently been left out of Wiccan thought because we don't seem to fit neatly into the notions of male-female polarity. This is based on erroneous assumptions that have also been used to stereotype gay men in other arenas. We're not masculine enough. We don't like or relate to women. We want to be women. We don't contribute to the creation of children. The list goes on and on.

All of these things are complete nonsense. There are as many different types of gay men as there are different types of people. The idea that we cannot, as Sybil Leek said, ever wholly participate in Witchcraft because we don't have the same connection to the "Life Force" Leek is so fond of discussing is utter garbage.

What is true is that it is easier to work with people whose personalities complement your own. Perhaps for the heterosexual Witches who defined the movement early on, the idea of working with same-gender people (whether homosexual or not) was for whatever reasons upsetting. Perhaps they simply didn't consider us because no gay people had ever made themselves known in Wiccan circles. I don't know, and it doesn't really matter. What matters is how gay men fit into the world of Witchcraft now.

I was surprised, when I first began studying Wicca, to discover that homophobia was rampant in the Witch community. Like many people who initially view Wicca as a big, happy wonderland open to everyone, I assumed that gay men would be welcome with open arms. This wasn't the case. In fact, at the first few gatherings I attended I discovered that gay men were more often seen as intruders to be tolerated rather than people who had something to contribute to the discussion.

This isn't to say that all the Witches I encountered were like this by any means, but enough were that I began to wonder why a spiritual path that supposedly was so open and loving seemed resistant to gay men. It reminded me, oddly enough, of the horror and fantasy writing world, which I am occasionally involved in because of some of the books I write for teenagers. In these communities, gay men are frequently shunned and sometimes outwardly attacked. At the very least, we are often merely tolerated.

What these worlds have in common, I believe, is a sizeable portion of the population that fears being suspect to outsiders. Already involved in what many people would consider unusual or even questionable practices (Witchcraft and genre writing), some people fear being perceived as even more peculiar by being tarnished with the stain of gayness. "If people know he's gay," they think, "they might think I'm gay, too."

It's a typical, generally heterosexual male, response, and one that gay men encounter throughout their lives in one form or another. In the case of Wicca, the result is that gay men, while welcomed by some groups, are more often than not either ignored or allowed to participate only in supporting roles within Wiccan circles.

I realize that I'm painting with a broad brush here, and I don't mean to imply that the entire Witch community effectively excludes gay men. There certainly are groups—the Reclaiming Tradition, for example—that actively involve gay men. But by and large, gay men have seldom had groups of their own in which to work. We have, as we have so many times, had to make do with what we can find.

So here I am, after railing against those who insist on working only in male-female pairs, suggesting that gay men need their own Wiccan groups. Yes, I am. I think that there is enormous power in coming together as gay men and forming our own circles. Why? Because we often have common experiences that provide us with an established base from which to begin our magical work.

Throughout history, gay people have always tried to make room for themselves within religious traditions. Virtually every one of the world's spiritual traditions now has some kind of gay-oriented group within it, from Catholicism to Islam, Buddhism to Evangelical Christianity. More often than not, these groups are not particularly welcome. But they exist because the women and men involved in them know that, despite what any of the so-called leaders of the faiths say, they have a right to seek spiritual truth in any way they please. No woman or man, and certainly no man-made law, can keep us from the divine, and when we understand this, it is incredibly freeing.

When I founded the Green Men, I did so because I was not satisfied with the Wiccan groups I'd found in my area. Although I enjoyed participating in some of their rituals, something was missing, and for me that was the ability to work with other people who shared some of my experiences. I wanted a group where I could feel comfortable being myself and where we could create an atmosphere for everyone to feel that way.

The men who became the Green Men were as different as could be. Some were effeminate and shy, while others were aggressive and domineering. Some were contemplative, while others preferred action to discussion and meditation. We each had our own personalities, our own strengths and weaknesses, our own reasons for being part of the group. Honestly, there were some members I would not have been friends with were it not for the group, such were their personalities. Yet, we all came together and it worked. Why? Because we had a common goal: to create a circle of gay men in which we would use our experiences to explore Pagan spirituality.

I have been in circles with straight men, straight women, and lesbians. I have been in mixed groups with other gay people. All of these experiences have been positive in some way. And frankly, when I first conceived of the idea for a circle of gay men, I was surprised. In general, I've always gotten along better with women and straight men than I have with other gay men. But something inside told me to try this, and since I had committed myself to going where I felt my path was leading me, I tried it.

Doing it changed my life, as I believe it did the lives of the other men involved. For one thing, it forced me to confront my own fears and misconceptions about other gay men. More important, it showed me how powerful it can be when people with a common purpose come together.

Since leaving Boston and the Green Men five years ago, I

have not been involved with another all-gay group. My practice is largely solitary now, primarily because of time constraints. But I still believe wholeheartedly that such groups can be wonderful places for gay men to discover much about themselves, and as I learn more and more about the path of Wicca, the more I am convinced that it's time for a gay revolution within the Craft.

Within the Pagan world at large, gay men have made their presence known in many ways. In particular, the loosely organized network of Radical Faerie groups have provided a welcoming home for gay men (and anyone else) interested in exploring Pagan spirituality. And more and more, classes and events for gay men are showing up on the calendars of Wiccan groups. This is encouraging, but I feel that more fully structured groups specifically for gay men are also needed.

I consider the Path of the Green Man a new tradition, a way of celebrating and practicing Witchcraft through the eyes of gay men. Certainly, the ideas in this book can be used by either individuals or groups. But why shouldn't gay men have their own tradition? I know there are many men who, like myself, spent a lot of years trying to fit into other people's groups. It's nice to have your own.

But is there really such a thing as gay Wicca? Are there gay deities, gay rituals, and gay ways of doing things? To a degree. But that's not really the point. The point is that whatever rituals are being done, whatever deities are being worked with, and whatever magic is being worked, it's being done by gay men, and that makes it unique. Also, the whole point of Wicca is understanding our lives and how we fit into the larger world. As gay men, we do occupy a unique place in the world, and acknowledging this is important.

When I first conceived of the Green Men, I wanted there to be some basic agreement on what we were doing and why.

To this end, I drafted what became known as the Green Man Manifesto, consisting of three parts: a Statement of Belief, a Statement of Purpose, and Principles of Unity. The Manifesto is reprinted here. You will notice that nowhere do the words *Witchcraft* or *Wicca* appear in the Manifesto. When we began, we were a group of men coming from often radically different spiritual backgrounds. We did not consider ourselves a coven as such, and so it was decided to use the word *Pagan* in discussing our activities. The guiding principles of the Green Men can certainly be used by those who do not choose to call themselves Witches or Wiccan. In fact, in some ways our core beliefs differ from traditional Wicca, particularly in that we view the Goddess and God as more or less equal personalities. Be that as it may, I believe that as a tradition of Witchcraft, Green Man Wicca stands as a more-than-valid addition to the ways in which the Craft is practiced.

You will also note that it is the Green *Man* Manifesto and not Green Men. This is because I always intended for the basic principles used by the group to apply equally to the individuals within it. Each of us is on our own journey, even when we travel together, and I never wanted us to forget that we are each the Green Man.

The Green Man Manifesto
Drafted on the night of November 15, 1998

Statement of Belief

The Green Men is a circle of gay-identified men who seek to integrate the practices and philosophies of Pagan spirituality and magic with the work of our everyday lives for the purpose of creating community and effecting change in ourselves and in the world. While many of us may also work within other traditions and groups, we believe there is a need for and a value to a circle comprised specifically of gay men walking the Pagan path. We see our sexuality as a blessing from the Goddess and God, and find value and importance in creating a circle where the unique joys and fears, concerns and gifts of gay men and their lives can be celebrated. Our membership is, therefore, limited to men who are gay identified, while continuing to recognize the equal importance of all peoples and beliefs.

Statement of Purpose

The purpose of the Green Men is threefold:

One—to form a loving community of gay Pagan men that sustains its members and provides a safe forum for creating lasting, positive friendships.

Two—to explore our own lives and our own spiritual journeys in concrete ways through questioning and learning, ritual and magic, art and sharing, with the goal of expanding awareness and consciousness and becoming more centered people.

Three—to integrate our spirituality into our everyday lives in a way that reflects our belief that we are all a part of a larger interconnected web and are able to effect positive change in the world in which we live.

Principles of Unity

As a way of creating a basis for our community, we have established the following Principles of Unity:

1. We believe in the fundamental truth of the Rede: "An It Harm None, Do As You Will" as it applies to our workings.

2. We believe in the guiding power of the Goddess and the God, who work in harmony. We acknowledge the Goddess as the bestower of life, and the God as the manifestation of the magic and life force of the natural world. We recognize that both the Goddess and God appear in many different forms and under many different names, and see the joyful celebration of deity in all its forms as valid and life-affirming.

3. We acknowledge the sacredness of the Earth as the living body of the Goddess and the home of the God, and dedicate ourselves to protecting the land, air, and water from harm caused by others and by our own actions. As part of this, we accept the gifts of the four elements of Earth, Air, Fire, and Water and recognize them as our guides.

4. We acknowledge all women and men as children of the God and Goddess, and dedicate ourselves to speaking out against injustice, bigotry, and hatred against any people, knowing that they are a part of ourselves.

5. We acknowledge the sacred gift of our sexuality, and accept our queerness as a special manifestation of the loving nature of the God, vowing not to use our sexual gifts to cause harm to others.

6. We believe in making our daily lives outward manifestations of our spiritual journeys, and endeavor to create lives that celebrate the abundant gifts of the Goddess and God and that return to our communities, and to the larger world, some of what we have been given.

7. We believe in the existence of magic and the power of ritual, and dedicate ourselves to learning their mysteries as they apply to our lives.

8. We believe in the beauty and power of intentional com-

munity, and strive to create a loving extended community, based in friendship, of gay men.

9. We believe that each man has a life story to tell and that the sharing of these stories makes us stronger and brings joy to the God and Goddess. To always remind ourselves of this, we vow that things spoken of by members during circles and meetings will stay within those places.

10. We recognize the beauty and power of song, story, poetry, and art that celebrates the Goddess and God and that reflects both our own stories and those of others, and we dedicate ourselves to the creation of art in all its forms.

11. We recognize the wisdom and power of elder men, and celebrate the gifts they have to bestow on us if we are wise enough to ask for them.

12. We believe in the effectiveness of community cooperation and will strive for equal participation by all interested members in decision making and in the creation of rituals and circles.

13. We recognize the importance of place and home and dedicate ourselves to working toward the creation of physical sanctuaries and homes for gay men interested in working in the Green Man tradition.

While all parts of the manifesto are important to me, I am particularly proud of placing numbers 11 and 13 into our Principles of Unity. One of the most important lessons I learned from attending a Reclaiming Tradition Witch Camp was the importance of learning from one another, and particularly of learning from elders. Too often in the gay community older men are shunted aside and perceived as unworthy of notice. It's vitally important that we change that attitude, and there's no better place to start than in our spiritual journeys. I have learned more from older gay men in my life than I have from any books. They are sources of enormous inspiration to me, and I value the friendship of my older friends more and more with each passing year.

Number 13 was inspired by my limited but incredibly rewarding experiences with the Radical Faeries. Several Faerie communities exist throughout the world, where you can go to participate in retreats, revive the spirit, and commune with other like-minded individuals. At the time I wrote the Green Man Manifesto, the latest Faerie community, called Faerie Camp Destiny, was coming together in Vermont. I had met some of the Vermont Faeries during my time at Witch Camp and was greatly impressed by their ability to create sustainable communities out of what at first glance appeared to be complete chaos.

At the time of this writing, no physical Green Men communities have been created, but I do maintain the hope that someday there will be a place where men interested in the Green Man tradition can come together. Perhaps, like the Reclaiming Traditions Witch Camps, there will be annual Green Men events where gay men can gather to celebrate our spiritual quests and learn from one another.

But even if the principles of the Green Men are practiced solely in living rooms and forest glens, dorm rooms and apartments, that is enough. While I do believe that the principles of the Green Man tradition can be the basis for a complete spiritual life, I also believe that these principles can be used in conjunction with other spiritual traditions as well.

Although it is becoming more common as Pagan parents raise their children in their traditions, very few people are born into Wicca. That means most of us come to it from other spiritual backgrounds. For some people, divesting themselves of the notion that you "are" whatever spiritual tradition you were born into or raised in can be difficult. This is particularly true for people from spiritual traditions in which ethnicity or cultural identity are heavily tied into a particular spirituality. People from Catholic and Jewish backgrounds, for example, may feel stronger pressure to maintain these identities because of how inextricably the spiritual tenets of these faiths are part of a larger identity.

If you are someone who is seeking to explore spirituality beyond the realm of your past or current faith, it's important to know why you're seeking change. Too often, we run from our spirituality because of anger or frustration, hoping that something else will provide us with what we're looking for. Although this is completely understandable, it may not always be the best path for us.

I was raised in the Baptist faith. As part of my religious schooling, I was told that there were certain things I needed to believe if I was to truly be a Christian. In particular, I was taught that I had to accept the fact that Jesus Christ was sacrificed through crucifixion to atone for the sins of humankind. There were other things that went along with this: for example, the belief that Jesus was the son of God and born of a virgin, the existence of Satan, and the absolute truth of the Bible. If I didn't believe these things, and if I didn't recognize that I was inherently a sinner who was doomed to an eternity in hell without the saving grace of Christ, I didn't stand a chance.

In addition to these "facts" that I was told to accept, I was led to believe that there were certain ways that good Christians behaved. We did not smoke or drink. We did not engage in lustful thoughts, and most certainly not in adultery. When I was a child, good Baptists also did not get divorced. If I obeyed these rules, I would be happy.

As I grew older, I started to take a closer look at the people who were telling me these things, and I discovered something interesting. Although they were telling me that if I did what they told me to I would be happy, they didn't seem awfully happy themselves. Even more interesting, as the years went on they seemed to change the rules, often when something they wanted to do had hitherto been forbidden. When a number of church members began to seek divorce, for example, suddenly it became time for the leaders to "reexamine" their stance on that issue.

My disillusionment with my faith came in two stages. The first stage involved feeling betrayed by the people who had been my teachers. Here, they had been telling me that if I did what they said, my life would be happy and I would be content. But I wasn't, despite frequently beating myself up over perceived transgressions of the laws and attempting to get back on track. Also, they clearly weren't happy, and if they weren't happy living the way they said I was to live, how could what they say be trusted?

The second stage of separation occurred some time later and was fundamentally more important. This involved having to decide whether or not I believed the basic tenets of Christianity. I'd already decided the Baptist faith wasn't for me, but I thought that perhaps it was simply that take on Christianity that didn't appeal to me. There were other options, lots of them, and I decided to give it another go, this time with the Episcopal Church.

For a time, I was happy. As I mentioned previously, I even applied to the seminary. But at some point I began to look— really look—at what I was being asked to accept. Did I, I asked myself, really believe that God had produced a son through

Mary? Did I believe that that son died as a sacrifice, and that by accepting his forgiveness my soul could be spared from eternal separation from God?

No, I decided, I didn't believe those things. I loved the stories of the Bible. I loved the message of Jesus Christ. But certain things about the whole business troubled me. I could almost—but not quite—get into the idea that God had sacrificed his son for the good of humankind. What I couldn't get over, though, was the notion that God would condemn anyone who didn't recognize him as the supreme creator. There were other things, too, but that was the main one. Quite simply, it seemed downright meanspirited of him to create humankind and then turn around and give us an "or else."

There are many people who, like myself, have trouble with various aspects of Christianity. Many of them have made room for themselves in the faith by accepting certain parts and leaving others behind. For me that wasn't enough. I wanted something I *could* believe in, and so I was off on a spiritual journey to find it.

Buddhism worked for a while, but frankly I found its rejection of almost everything to be a little tiring. I needed something a little more lively, a little less stoic. And that brought me to Paganism and Wicca. It works for me. And it's here that I find the most fulfilling exploration of my spirituality.

Do I believe that Jesus Christ existed? I like to think he did, and I like to think that his message of peace and love changed the lives of the people who heard it. But I don't like what the religion founded on his teachings has turned into. Do I believe that Buddha and Mohammed existed? Again, I have no reason not to believe that. And I respect anyone who genuinely finds spiritual happiness and life-changing experiences within any of these traditions.

If you're feeling discouraged by a particular spiritual path, it's important to examine whether it's the actual tenets of that path that you have difficulty accepting or the people promoting those tenets. Spirituality is not something you change like a shirt or your hair color. It is—or should be—a deeply personal choice that is made after sincere thought and real examination of what is important to you and what you believe.

There is a lot of talk these days about the watering-down of spirituality to make it accessible to as many people as possible. There are even some people who put forth the idea that a person is more or less stuck with whatever religion he or she is born into because to fully become part of a faith you must be part of the community and culture from which it sprang. I partially agree with some of these arguments, in the sense that I do believe too many of us create spiritual rules that fit how we want to behave, not how we should behave. As to the suggestion that you are whatever you were born as, I really couldn't disagree more strongly. I believe we find our spirituality where we find it, regardless of color, gender, nationality, or anything else. I have met non-African people who have experienced tremendous personal change by participating in traditional African religions, lifelong Catholics who have rediscovered the joy of spirituality after converting to Judaism, and even Wiccans who have found their paths taking them into the world of Buddhism.

If you are someone coming to this book in search of something that works for you spiritually, welcome. Whatever you find here is yours for the taking. All I ask is that you approach your exploration of these principles with respect and with a full understanding of the thought behind them. Also, remember that whatever faith we hold we are, most of us, looking for the same thing.

IN THE HOUSE OF BRIGID

A Story for Imbolc

ABOUT IMBOLC

In Celtic mythology, Brigid (pronounced "breed") is the goddess of fire, poetry, and inspiration. On the night of Imbolc, also called Candlemas, bonfires are lit on the tops of hills all over Ireland and parts of England to celebrate her gifts.

Imbolc itself means "in the belly." At Yule we celebrate the rebirth of the sun. At Imbolc the light renewed at Yule has quickened in the belly of the Earth, who will then give birth at the next sabbat, Ostara, the spring equinox.

Traditionally, Imbolc is a time to look for what inspires us in our work of the coming year and what is preventing us from creating these things we desire to bring to life. Brigid's fire becomes both a place of releasing when we give up to it that which we wish to sacrifice and a place of creation when we allow its warmth to suffuse our souls and our lives and kindle the spark of creativity.

EVER SO SLOWLY, the winter passed. Each night, as he sat before the fire, the Green Man continued to look into the stone given to him by the Horned God on the longest night. He told the stone the story of his life, and each day he saw the light within it shining more brightly than the day before. He also saw that, as the Lord of the Green Wood had promised, the sun began to tarry longer in the sky each day.

At the turn of the year, the Green Man watched the skies as the moon came twice to fullness. Shortly after its second rising, he became restless. He felt that beneath the skin of cold the blood of the Earth was beginning to stir once more. Even though the winds still howled and the snow continued to fall, he sensed in the world about him the first promise of waking. As he walked the woods around his home, he found himself looking forward to the time when the leaves would cover the thin branches and the first flowers would burst through the dark, rich earth.

But still there was much snow and cold. As he looked ahead to the coming season, the Green Man began to worry. His heart was filled with growing warmth. His head was full of dreams he longed to bring to life and work he hoped to see begun. Yet, he feared that he would not be able to do it. Having lent all of who he was to the task of calling back the sun, he doubted his ability to give any more. He wondered if, in his desire, he had used up his own fire.

One night, as the Green Man stood at his window looking out on the moonlit snow and wondering what the turning of the Wheel of the Year would bring, he saw something on one of the hills. At the very top, where the snow gave way to black sky, there was a flicker of light. The Green Man stared at it, wondering who or what had made the fire. Then he saw another flame, on a hill farther on, and then another.

Wrapping himself in his cloak, the Green Man took up his walking stick and left his house. His feet made quick time through the snow as he walked into the hills, keeping the fire always within his sight. The night was clear and the winds still, and the flame burned strong and bright. As he walked, it grew larger and larger, until he was walking up the very hill on which the fire sat.

He was surprised, on reaching the summit, to find the fire tended by a girl. She was young, no more than a maiden, and as she carefully added sticks to the fire she hummed a faint song.

"Who might you be?" asked the Green Man. He thought himself all alone in his valley, and the sight of the girl puzzled him. She wore a red cloak, and her hair fell freely about her shoulders.

The girl looked at him with eyes that shone in the night. "I light the way to the house of Brigid," she said simply. "Will you go there?"

The Green Man had no answer for her, having never before heard the name of which she spoke. But no matter what he asked, he could get no more from her. He knew of no house other than his own and thought that surely the girl was mistaken. Yet, he saw further on another fire, and something within in him urged him toward it.

He climbed another hill and again found himself in front of a fire. It was tended by a woman older than the first, a mother whose belly was quick with child. She, too, wore a red cloak, but her hair was wrapped in a single braid that fell down her back. As she added sticks to her fire, she sang the same song as the girl had done.

"What is your name?" the Green Man asked. "And what are you about?"

The mother smiled at him. "I light the way to the house of Brigid," she said. "Will you go there?" And no matter how he begged, she would tell him no more.

Again he walked, and again he came to the top of a hill. This third fire was tended by a crone. Her cloak of red covered her head, and he saw only shadows of her face as she bent to add sticks to her fire, which despite her age and slowness burned as brightly as those of the other two. Her work, too, was accompanied by a song, although the singing of it was worn to the barest thread of a melody.

"Can you tell me, grandmother, what you do here?" the Green Man asked.

"I light the way to the house of Brigid," she said simply. "Will you go there?"

The Green Man looked to the next hill, but he saw no more fires burning. Nor did he see any house.

"Where is the way?" he asked the crone in despair. He had come far and was weary. Although he knew not who Brigid was, his heart was filled with a desire to reach her.

The crone lifted one hand and pointed to a place between two hills. There, where no house had been before, the Green Man saw a cottage. Its windows were golden with light and the door was open.

He hurried through the snow, anxious to come to the door, and soon he stood outside the cottage. From within he heard the sound of singing, and he forgot the coldness of the night and the tiredness of his body.

Entering through the open door, the Green Man found himself in a room filled with the warmth of a fire and the light of a thousand candles. The air rang with the sound of song, and he soon realized that it was the same beautiful melody he had heard sung by the three guardians of the fires. Only now the song rang clear as a bell and golden as the sun through the house, as though it were a living thing rejoicing in all of creation.

He looked for the source of the music, but saw neither players nor singers. He saw only that in the center of the room was a fire, the smoke from which escaped through a hole in the roof in thick tangles. Around it danced a woman. She was dressed in cloth of red and gold, and she swirled and swayed around the flames as though she were part of the fire herself. Even her hair was both red and gold together, and it flew about her shoulders as she danced. Her face reflected the light of the fire, and looking at her, the Green Man knew that he was in the home of Brigid.

She ceased her dancing and stood before him. "Welcome to my house," she said, and her voice was like music and fire.

The Green Man removed his cloak and bowed. Brigid laughed.

"You need not bow to me," she said. "But answer me this: What have you come for?"

The Green Man was puzzled. He had been so filled with the need to reach this place that now that he was here, he could not think of what it was he sought. Brigid stood, watching his face and staring at him with eyes like stars.

The Green Man closed his eyes. He felt the warmth of the house fill him, he listened to the song that still played, and he knew then what he wanted.

"Inspiration," he said. "The strength to create and to build and to grow. The strength I feel in this house."

Brigid laughed. "But you already have those things within you," she said.

The Green Man did not understand. Inside he felt the force of his passion blocked by fear and worry. He feared that his hopes, when birthed, would look nothing as they did in his dreams. He saw in his mind a vision of his life and worried that the reality would be far from what he wished for. While he longed for the warmth of spring, he was not sure if, when it came, he could bring into being the things he planned during the long nights of darkness.

"I am afraid," he said simply, and even in the warm light of the thousand candles he felt suddenly very cold.

"Come," said Brigid, "warm yourself at the fire."

The Green Man stepped forward, and as he did, the fire was extinguished. The last remnants of smoke escaped through the roof, and at the same time the song that filled the house was silenced. He looked at the logs, thick with soot, and he wept at the loss.

"Do not cry," said Brigid. "The fire can easily be rekindled. But it is you who must do it."

"But how?" asked the Green Man, who saw in the ruins of the fire the ashes of his dreams.

"Give to it the things that you fear, the things that hold you back, the things that prevent your heart from being light," said Brigid.

The Green Man looked into his heart. He saw there fear of failure, shame, and anger. He discovered doubt, worry, and condemnation. All the time he had been trying to call forth the light, while he had been dreaming and planning, they had been secretly trying to dismantle that which he constructed, tugging at the stones and weakening the foundation. He had let their criticizing voices fill his ears with lies, thinking them to be the voices of reason. But now, in the light of Brigid's house, he saw them for what they were: pale, weak things that fed on his light.

He took these things and pulled them from his heart. Though they tried to cling to him, he brought them into the light, where they writhed in his hands. He held them above the cold remnants of the fire and offered them up to it. When they touched the wood, they sparked, and the sparks rekindled the fire. Soon, it was burning brightly again, and the warmth returned to the house, as did the music and song, which he understood now was birthed in the heart of Brigid's fire.

"Thank you," said Brigid. "You have given up what you found hardest to give. And in return, you will fill yourself with the wonder of my fire."

Taking his hand, she knelt with the Green Man at the side of her fire and bade him peer into it. At first, his eyes were blinded by the light inside the flames. It flashed gold, orange, and white, dizzying him. But as he continued to look, the light cleared, and soon he saw that Brigid's fire was filled with the beauty of creation.

"Reach in," she told him. "Take what you find there."

The Green Man trembled as he placed his hand into the fire, fearing it would burn him. But his skin was not harmed, and when he withdrew his hand he saw that he held in his palm the word *spirit*. It sat on his palm for a moment and then lifted into the air, circling about his head like a great golden dragonfly.

"Take another," urged Brigid, and once more the Green Man reached into her fire.

This time he emerged with the word *choice*. It, too, became a flicker of light that encircled him.

Several times Brigid told the Green Man to draw a word from her fire, and each time he found in his hand another gift. Soon, Brigid's words swarmed around him as moths around a light. He felt them filling him with their power, and he spoke them aloud: spirit, choice, growth, laughter, kindness, change. Each one gave to him something of itself.

"These are your gifts," Brigid told him. "And now it is up to you to use them."

From the corner of her house she brought the Green Man a pot of dirt and a handful of seeds. She placed the seeds in his hand.

"Take each one," she said. "Speak into it one of your strengths and one of your dreams. Then plant it in the soil."

The Green Man took a seed and held it to his lips. "Song," he whispered into it. Then he told the seed one of his most precious dreams, and he pushed it into the pot of earth.

He took another, and spoke another word and another dream into it. Soon, the pot was filled with the seeds of his intentions. Brigid held it out before her and spoke.

"Tend your seeds," she said. "As you care for them, they will grow. And as they grow, your dreams will flower with them. But remember: you must care for them. Give to them freely of yourself and they will reward you with beauty. Otherwise, they will die."

The Green Man took the pot of dreams and held it to him. Within it, he felt his visions taking shape. He knew that the seeds held the power of Brigid's words and of his own desires.

Thinking of them taking root in the soil, he felt his own resolve deepen, reaching down into his depths to take hold.

"Remember also to feed yourself," Brigid said. "Just as the seeds need tending, so do you. Feed yourself well on the things that nourish you, on song and poetry and love. Create with your hands and with your voice. Dance and sew and build. Open yourself to the gifts of my inspiration, and you will find that you can never exhaust them. And just as your fears became the sparks that stirred my fire, let them be that which drives you through the remaining time of darkness and into the new season. They are the soil from which new life springs. Give them up and let them be recycled into the web of birth and death and rebirth."

For the remainder of the night the Green Man stayed with Brigid. She fed him well from her kitchen, and he shared with her his hopes for the future as they danced together. But before dawn, he fell asleep near her fire, where he dreamed of songs he would sing, stories he would write, and gardens he would plant. When he awoke, he found himself on top of a hill, looking down at his house in the valley. Beside him were the remains of a fire, but the house of Brigid was gone. The pot of seeds he had planted sat nearby. He picked it up, and as he held it in his hands he heard again the words of power he had plucked from Brigid's fire. They stirred in the earth, and in his mind, and he remembered his promise to keep them safe and well.

As the Green Man began the long walk back to his home, the words danced in his head, forming and reforming themselves into snatches of song and lines of poetry. When he arrived home, he placed the pot of seeds in his sunniest window, sat down before it, and began to write down all that he had seen and done during the night.

Chapter 3

The Wiccan Worldview

Every spiritual path has two primary elements to it: the principles that define it and the activities that are the expression of these principles. Christianity, for example, has as one of its core beliefs the death and resurrection of Jesus Christ. The expression of this belief is Communion, in which participants ritually partake of the "body" and "blood" of Christ.

Witchcraft is no different. There are basic beliefs of Wicca that need to be thoroughly understood before you can fully engage in the rituals of the path. Although these beliefs will be strengthened by participation in the accompanying rituals and will deepen over time, no exploration of Witchcraft is possible without knowing something about what it all means.

As we've already discussed, there is no formal set of rules that Witches follow. The Wiccan Rede is the closest thing to any commandment or edict that exists in the Craft. It says "An it harm none, do as you will." The easy—and lazy—way to interpret the Rede is that anything you want to do is okay as long as it doesn't harm anyone or anything. To take it this way, however, is to ignore the deeper meanings of Witchcraft.

There is another belief of Wicca, generally called the Law of Three, which states that any energy (meaning intention, action, or purpose) you send out into the world will eventually come back to you three times as strong. Taken in conjunction with the Rede, this is a pretty good summary of Wiccan thought.

But what, really, does it mean? It should be fairly obvious that harming living things is wrong. But what constitutes "harm"? What does it mean that your intentions come back to you three times as forcefully as when you sent them out? And how do you "send" out energy anyway? Some of these things we'll discuss in more depth in chapter 5. Right now we need to talk a bit about Wiccan theology.

Most religions have fairly lengthy sets of rules about what's right and wrong. Witchcraft doesn't. Primarily this is because Wicca is a spiritual tradition based on personal responsibility. In most faiths, failing to obey the rules results in angering some kind of higher power. In Witchcraft, we believe that we are all part of the same web, everything connected to everything else, everyone responsible for the well-being of the whole.

If you accept this notion of the world, you begin to see how your actions will, eventually, come back to affect you. I like to think of it as a ripple effect. When I do something, the consequences of that action ripple out, sometimes in small circles and sometimes in large ones. As these circles expand, they come to encompass other people, whose lives are then also affected by what I've done. Eventually, the ripples I've started will begin to come back toward me, bringing with them the magnified effects of my actions. Obviously, when I find myself in the path of these ripples, I want whatever they carry to be benevolent and peaceful.

Okay, so this might sound like a lot of New Agey horse shit, right? And it's quite a responsibility to have the life of every living thing in the world connected to you. After all, you didn't ask to be tied to, say, some six-year-old kid in India who you have nothing to do with.

Sorry, but you do. We live in a time when personal responsibility isn't a very popular notion. It's easier to turn away from things that are troubling, to ignore things that "aren't our problem" and let other people deal with them. Well, frankly, that's how we got where we are in the first place. Seeing yourself as the center of the universe may make you feel better about yourself, but living with that kind of attitude has an enormous impact on the world as a whole.

Take, for example, the increasingly common business practice of outsourcing jobs to countries where the workers are paid lower wages than they are elsewhere. To the people looking at the bottom line of the business, this makes perfect sense. Lower costs means more profit, which makes stockholders happy and the company "successful." Perhaps they even justify their actions to themselves by saying that because of their cost-cutting measures, they can offer whatever their product is to consumers at a reduced rate. To the workers who get the new jobs, it might look like a great thing as well. They're working. They're making money for their families.

But what is the real cost of this kind of practice? First, some workers lose their jobs. They can't afford to support their families. More than that, they feel devalued because they discover that they've been seen as things rather than as people, things that have no intrinsic value other than their ability to make a company's product. Second, the new workers who get the jobs certainly do experience some benefits. But they also find themselves part of a machine that, for the most part, has no interest in their wellfare. They aren't encouraged to look beyond whatever job it is they perform. They aren't encouraged to create real change in themselves or their communities. They simply fill a need.

What if, instead of looking at the bottom line purely in terms of numbers, businesses measured their success in terms of how much impact they have on the lives of the people they employ? Imagine how that would change things. For example, I have a friend who owns a bakery. Her bakery has become extremely profitable due to its relationship with a national chain of coffeehouses for which my friend produces baked goods.

It would be easy for this woman to simply take the money she makes and put it in the bank. It would be easy for her to cut quality and still maintain her contracts and increase her take. But she doesn't. Instead, she has chosen to use her business to make dramatic changes in the lives of the people who work for her. The workers—most of them uneducated women and men who have been overlooked by traditional employers—have a strong say in the business. They hold positions of leadership, and they are encouraged to learn how everything works. Equally important, my friend makes sure that a substantial portion of the bakery's earnings are used for the education of her workers and their families. They are not told to be satisfied with what she's made possible for them; they are encouraged to look beyond it, to discover what it is they want from their lives and to find ways of achieving these things.

My friend is not a Witch, but she beautifully exemplifies the principles of Witchcraft. She very much enjoys the success she has, but she knows that it is just as important to use her success to make life better for other people. She is one of the happiest people I know, and I believe this is due in large part to the fact that she understands her place in the web of the world.

It's easy to scapegoat big businesses, and I realize that. Nor am I suggesting that there is a way to make everyone equal. Some of us have economic, educational, and societal advantages that others don't. And certainly people are entitled to make successes of themselves. But it's just as important that we understand how the choices we make, whether they be in our business or personal lives, affect others.

Let's look at a more dramatic example of this principle in action. After the attacks on the United States on September 11, 2001, we found ourselves bombarded with information about what had happened and why. Very quickly, things were condensed to a simplistic explanation: America had been attacked by Muslim extremists because the terrorists saw us as a threat to their beliefs. Things escalated into an Us versus Them situation, with flag waving, protests, and demands for justice on all sides.

I happened to be having some furniture delivered to my house on the day of the attacks. It was early in the morning, and I was, like most people in the country, watching CNN and waiting for the full story to be pieced together. I'd totally forgotten about the couch and chairs that were on their way.

When the doorbell rang, I opened it to find two men, clearly of Arab descent, standing there with my delivery. They walked in, carrying the couch between them. They stopped in the middle of the living room and stared at the television, where the footage of the World Trade Center buildings collapsing was playing over and over. Apparently, neither man knew anything had happened. They stood for a full five minutes or so, still holding the couch, just staring at the television screen.

Finally, they put the couch down. "What have we done?" one of them asked, looking at me with tears in his eyes.

His question could be interpreted several ways, depending on who you are and what your viewpoint is. He could have been speaking as a Muslim, but he could just as easily have been speaking as an American. The events that led to what happened on September 11 are far too complex to blame on any one group, and we could debate for years why what happened occurred.

Forget what led to the attacks and think instead about

everyone whose lives were affected by the choices made on and *after* September 11. First, there were the immediate dead, their families, and the people of New York City, tens of thousands of people whose lives were forever altered by the actions of people they didn't even know. As the days went by, the ripple that began when that first plane crashed into the side of a tower in downtown New York spread, growing wider and wider until it contained not just New York, not just the East Coast, not just the United States, but the entire world.

Even now those ripples continue out, drawing more and more people in. The United States went to war against Iraq. Thousands of people have died. Hundreds of thousands more have had their lives irrevocably changed in ways that can never be undone. If you compare the number of people directly affected on September 11 to the number affected since then, the Law of Three seems to be very much in effect.

It would be easy to look at this situation and say that certain things in it are good and certain things are bad. It would be easy—and has been easy for many people—to point fingers and lay blame. But the underlying truth is that certain people made choices and those choices affected the entire world in one way or another.

As a Wiccan looking at September 11, I found myself thinking more than ever about the idea that we are all connected. A friend from my childhood—a girl I went to my first rock concert with (it was the Go-Go's, if you must know)—was killed in the Trade Center collapse, although I wouldn't discover that for almost two years after. Friends in New York were among those who exited subway stations that morning to find fire, metal, and bodies tumbling from the sky. When George W. Bush went to war with Iraq, some of the people he sent were the sons and daughters, wives and husbands of friends of mine.

Many of us made things easier on ourselves by saying that

we were going to war against terrorism. Not against people, but against a concept. It is easy to tell yourself that you aren't connected to something when it has no face, no real name, no eyes to stare back at you. But the truth is, we went to war against human beings.

What would have happened if instead of focusing on retaliation we tried to understand the actions and events that precipitated the violence? What was our real purpose in going to war against terrorism? These are questions that can't be answered, because we didn't choose these options. And responding to events like September 11 and those that came after is not easy. Am I relieved that Saddam Hussein is captured? Absolutely. Do I think the Iraqi people will be better off without him? No doubt. Do I think the way in which it was carried out is justified? No.

There is evil in the world. There are people who hurt just for the sake of hurting, and people who are hurt by others for no other reason than that they have no one to fight for them. I am not a pacifist. I am, in fact, quick to anger when I feel an injustice has been done. At the same time, I know these feelings need to be closely examined, that my motives for having them need to be closely examined lest they come to control me.

For example, I know that were I to encounter someone deliberately causing injury to an animal, I would not hesitate to beat the living tar out of that person. At the same time, I am wholeheartedly against the death penalty, because I don't believe that exacting revenge brings the peace that victims often believe it will. This is a contradiction in my character and something I think about often: this question of what, exactly, I feel the nature of justice is and when actions are and are not justified.

None of these questions are easy to answer, at least not for me. Earlier we discussed the Witch Starhawk and how her tradition, the Reclaiming Tradition, believes that Witches need to make the personal political. This is taking these fundamental beliefs of Wicca and making them the framework of your life. But how this is or isn't done is often a personal matter. For example, would the use of force be "right" if its purpose were to free people from a brutal, oppressive regime? That was certainly the excuse used by Bush in the attack on Iraq. But if freeing people from oppression is such a priority, why not intervene in other countries in the world where people are being mistreated and often murdered by their leaders? Why choose to intervene only when there is apparently some personal benefit to doing so?

If we are to live by the Wiccan Rede and the Law of Three, are committing actions that could potentially cause harm to others ever justified, even if the stated aim is to aid someone who needs it? I remember some years ago reading a posting made by a Witch on an online bulletin board regarding the way some Witches she knew were responding to a series of rapes that had occurred in the area in which they lived. One circle had held a ritual in which they envisioned sending out positive emotions to the rapist. Their reasoning was that if they could get the man to confront the anger that was causing him to rape, if he could feel that someone cared about what happened to him, he would stop.

The woman posting her response to this was furious. Instead of sending positive emotions the rapist's way, she wrote, they should be sending out energy to stop him in his tracks. She felt the response of her fellow Witches was passive aggressive and weak, that they were taking the Law of Three too literally.

What do you think? This is not an easy question to answer, just as the principles of Witchcraft are not always easy to live by, or even easy to define in one way or another. But that's exactly where the path lies. By exploring your responses to situations in which the Rede or the Law of Three applies, you discover who you are.

I once interviewed for a book I was writing a gentleman who was an elder in the Quaker tradition. This man was a life-long pacifist, a man whose father had given up a successful business career because his company became involved in making munitions for wartime use and who himself was one of the first conscientious objectors to military service based on religious principles. After discussing his beliefs for some time, I asked him, "What if someone were threatening your family?" There was a long pause, after which he replied, "I would hope that I am ready to be killed rather than kill. But I can't promise that."

Most of us like to believe that we have strong convictions and that we would be willing to stand up for these convictions. But how often are we really asked to? I have never had a loved one killed by someone else and been asked to condone or condemn the killer's own execution. Would I still be against the death penalty if I found myself in that situation? I honestly don't know. Would I feel differently about the actions taken against Iraq if instead of a childhood friend my partner had been killed on September 11? I don't know.

These are big questions, and hopefully ones that none of us will ever have to answer. But there are smaller examples that we are faced with on a daily basis, decisions we are asked to make that, if we truly believe in the Wiccan Rede and the Law of Three, provide regular opportunities for us to practice what we say we believe.

Take, for example, the issue of eating meat. Many Witches think that if you really believe in the Rede, you won't eat meat. Why? Most obviously because the production of meat involves the killing of a living creature, which I think anyone would agree constitutes doing it "harm." Beyond that, there are all the economic and environmental factors. Meat production is incredibly wasteful, using up valuable land that could be utilized for agriculture. Eating meat has been shown to contribute to various medical conditions. The arguments against meat consumption are many and compelling.

Other Witches disagree, arguing that eating meat is simply part of the natural world. There is a food chain, they reason, and it's just as much a part of nature as life and death, growth and decay. As long as we properly acknowledge the creatures from which our meat comes, and as long as we consume meat responsibly, then we are living by Wiccan principles.

I do happen to eat meat. I spent the majority of my adolescent and teen years in farm country. My family raised chickens, and every fall we had the Great Chicken Massacre, during which my father beheaded the birds and my mother and I feathered and gutted them. I have no illusions about chickens being intelligent, delightful birds. They are mean, smelly, stupid, and taste really good fried, especially accompanied by mashed potatoes.

I think this is one of the areas that I need to do a lot of work on myself. I agree with the idea that eating meat contributes to an unhealthy lifestyle and attitude about living things. I think factory farms are disgusting places. Most of all, I know that if my eating meat depended on my killing the animals myself, I would never do it. Well, maybe if it were a chicken, but definitely not a cow or pig.

Still, when I find myself at the grocery store, it's easy to forget these things, particularly if I'm hungry. Meat is easy. Besides, when it's all wrapped up and called beef instead of cow, or pork instead of pig, I can put the image of a terrified animal, a bolt gun or mallet coming toward its head, out of my mind and instead think nice thoughts about steak sauce and chops. Someone else has done the dirty work, after all. It's not as if I killed the poor thing.

Ah, but by buying and eating that meat, I'm saying that I approve of someone else raising an animal under inhumane conditions and killing it. My money is making it possible for someone to keep doing that. So am I responsible after all? Yes, I am.

So it's something I work on, and I'm getting better. When I look at meat in the store now, I force myself to acknowledge where it came from and under what conditions the animals whose meat I'm considering eating lived and died in. This is by no means a pleasant undertaking, particularly when my partner (who thinks this is all very silly) is standing there going, "Oh, for the love of God, are you thinking about how the cow had a mommy again?" But it's important to me to do this, important to me to try and change the way I eat because in some small way it will change the world I live in.

And that, ultimately, is what this is all about. It's unlikely that any of us are going to have the opportunity to change the world—either for good or bad—in a huge way, like Bush did when he decided to invade Iraq, or Adolf Hitler did when he convinced himself it was acceptable to attempt to wipe out an entire race of people, or Mohandas Gandhi did when he preached his message of nonviolence and helped his country escape British imperialism. Few of us are ever put into these positions.

We do have opportunities to make change, though. Maybe it's deciding not to eat meat. Perhaps it's deciding to help someone who needs it, choosing to speak out against a wrong we see being done in the world, or making choices that are responsible because they're the right one to make, if not the easy ones. Maybe these choices we make won't ever be noticed by anyone else. But we feel them inside ourselves, and bit by bit, they change how we walk through the world.

I don't have a lot of money to give to causes I think are worthwhile. Most of us don't. We can't buy the attention of a political leader, fund a research project, or pay to immunize every child in Africa against measles. And often we tell ourselves that if we can't fix the whole problem, there's not much point in involving ourselves in them. Besides, who has the time to march, volunteer, or write letters?

I decided several years ago that I would choose a couple of things I *could* do to help out and do them. They would be *my* things, my little ways of trying to send good things out into the universe. I began sponsoring, for a small sum each month, a child in India and a child in the United States. Also, I began donating money each month to a local marine wildlife refuge. I am an avid scuba diver, and I have a particular fondness for marine mammals, so this is a cause close to my heart.

I never have (and probably never will) meet any of the children I've sponsored. I like to think that their lives have been made a little better by my support, that maybe knowing someone they've never even met cares about them has helped them care more about themselves. Some of the marine mammals whose rehabilitation my contributions made possible I *have* met, and they were most definitely appreciative, at least if wet, fishy kisses are any indication.

These are small things, but it makes a difference that I do them. For each of us the things we do may be different. You may choose not to buy certain products based on the actions of the companies that produce them. Or alternatively, you may only buy products from companies you know do behave responsibly. I won't tell you that certain things are always right and certain things are always wrong. These decisions need to be made individually. But if, as someone interested in following the Wiccan path, you remember the words of the Rede and the concept of the Law of Three, I guarantee you that you'll find yourself making decisions differently and that you'll feel good about the choices you make.

As gay people, many of us are already well aware of the power our personal choices have. The gay community has made great advances by supporting pro-gay political candidates and campaigning against anti-gay ones. We've seen the power that comes from extending love and compassion to others, as evidenced most clearly in the many fine organizations that have sprung up to assist people affected by the AIDS crisis or by the support generated for victims of anti-gay violence. We know firsthand how positive, life-affirming choices can make a difference, both in the people we're reaching out to and, consequently, ourselves.

These are excellent examples of the Law of Three in action. Most people, when they volunteer for something, generally do so because they want to help someone else. But what most of us find is that by helping we get back far more than we give. Having written several books on the AIDS crisis, I've interviewed dozens of people who, either by choice or by circumstance, have been drawn into volunteering. To a person, these volunteers tell me that they've received so much more from their volunteer experiences than they ever thought possible. By giving of themselves, they've found that generosity returned to them many times over.

That's really what the Law of Three is all about. So, if putting positive energy and action into the world causes us to receive positive responses, how does the reverse work? Again, most of us have seen this in action too. How many people do you know complain endlessly about how unfair the world is to them or constantly blame their problems on other people? And how often do you see these same people's lives getting more and more bleak, more and more unhappy, as if they're drowning in a whirlpool of misery?

There are terrible things that happen to us that are absolutely not our fault. But there are also things that "happen" to us because we create an atmosphere around us that allows them to happen. Being abused as a child is not anyone's fault. Continuing to have abusive relationships as an adult is something we choose. Having an addiction is not necessarily our fault; choosing to let that addiction destroy us is.

We choose how we live our lives. Every day we make decisions about what and what not to do. If we make positive decisions, our lives will generally go in a positive direction. If we make negative, hurtful decisions, we build up a wall of negativity that makes it seemingly impossible for us to escape.

I once was on a trip with a group of people where one of the participants complained at great length about everything. He made the trip difficult to enjoy because of his consistently bleak outlook, and finally I lost my temper and told him that his behavior was really ruining the trip for everyone else. He looked at me in shock and said, "It must be nice to live in a world where everything is perfect."

I spent many months afterward hating this man. Every time I thought about him, I grew more and more angry. What possible reason, I wondered, could he have for being so absolutely miserable, and why did he feel the need to make everyone around him feel miserable as well? I congratulated myself on having shown him up and calling him on his behavior, even though secretly I wondered if maybe I hadn't behaved a little badly myself.

I'd almost forgotten about things when, almost a year later, it became the center of a larger controversy involving this same man when he had a run-in with someone else and the previous incident was brought up as evidence of his ongoing difficult behavior. A long, ugly fight ensued, causing everyone involved a lot of unhappiness. Again, I found myself indignantly wondering what was "wrong" with this man. Probably, I told myself (and anyone who would listen) he was just a hateful, terrible person, or at the very least he had a tiny penis and was making the rest of us pay for it.

I was ranting about this to a friend of mine one day. She listened patiently as I went on and on about how unfair all of this was, how terribly inconvenient and distressing and, well, annoying. "Someone should do something about him," I said forcefully.

"Have you ever thought that he might be terribly, terribly lonely?" my friend asked.

Law of Three or not, I wanted to smack her. That was the last thing I wanted to think about. That involved seeing this man as a human being instead of a monster. But as the days went on, I started to think maybe she was right. Okay, I *knew* she was right, but I needed a few days to let myself accept it.

Finally, I ended up having dinner with the man who was at the center of the storm in an attempt to defuse the situation. As we talked that night, I discovered that he was indeed very lonely. He was also smart and funny, and we shared a lot of things in common. I won't say that we became the best of friends, but I came away from that dinner understanding a lot more about him, and a lot more about myself. I was letting my anger at this person control how I related to him, and as a result the cloud of negativity surrounding me when it came to my relationship with him grew larger and larger, resulting in bigger and bigger problems. But by changing my approach to the situation, I was able to change its course.

This is what following the path of the Green Man does. It presents us with challenges, and how we meet these challenges determines what we learn about ourselves and the world. We certainly don't always succeed, at least not in the sense that we consistently make the right choices, but sometimes the perceived failures end up teaching us more than we ever thought possible.

Let's look at another real-life way in which the Wiccan Rede and the Law of Three can be applied to our lives. In this case, we'll talk about sex, a matter near and dear to the hearts of many of us. What does sex have to do with being a Green Man? Well, for one thing it's a perfect arena for employing our belief in the concepts of Witchcraft.

As mentioned earlier, Witchcraft encourages the exploration of all the positive things life has to offer, and this includes sex. Besides being integrally tied to the cycles of life and death, it's also a lot of fun. So what does the Rede or the Law of Three have to do with it?

Sex, whether casual or within a relationship, involves a lot of emotions that affect us on various levels, some of which we may not even be aware of. Where sex for one partner may simply be about getting off, for another it may have all kinds of other feelings attached to it. When we engage in sex with another person, we are contributing to whatever emotional experience he (and since this book is primarily for gay men, kindly excuse me for using the masculine pronouns) is having. Again, this may not be any big deal, but sometimes it is.

Who we choose to have sex with, and how we choose to express ourselves sexually, does have an effect on both ourselves and our partners. Treating sex casually (and by this I am referring to our attitudes toward sex, and not necessarily the way in which we engage in it) can be extremely damaging on an emotional level, and this is something that those of us who are sexually active need to keep in mind.

Take, for example, a man who regularly engages in anonymous sex. Is this necessarily a bad thing? Not at all. But what if he's doing it because he's avoiding confronting other issues in his life? Or what if the men he's having sex with are bringing their own issues into the mix. It's very easy to shove these things aside and say that they don't matter, but I think they do. I believe that the ways we conduct ourselves sexually can have a profound impact on the rest of our lives.

Again, I want to stress that I am not advocating against casual sex. I think casual sexual behavior can be an enormously positive experience when approached properly. What I am saying is that we need to consider the potential effects of how we behave sexually, of how what we do to or with others may affect them. Although we often call the image of the gay man who spends his life engaged in casual sexual encounters a stereotype, the fact is, many of us know men like that. We also know that these men are frequently not particularly happy. Most of us also know men who complain bitterly about not being able to find a lover, all the while treating the men they interact with as if they're no more important than a one-night stand.

The cumulative effect of this kind of behavior is not positive. First, you are doing your partners a disservice. Second, you are doing yourself a disservice. Think of it in terms of the Wiccan Rede. Are you harming anyone? On the surface, maybe you don't think so. But what if your sexual partner has a partner at home who doesn't know about his outside activities? Perhaps that isn't your responsibility, but aren't you in some way contributing to an unhealthy situation? What if your partner is seeking through sexual activity things he should be looking for elsewhere? Are you not in some way helping him continue to avoid things he needs to address?

As I've stated before, it all comes back to personal responsibility. No, you may not be directly responsible for someone else's choices and behavior, but you *are* responsible for putting yourself into a situation where you may, knowingly or not, be causing someone else emotional distress or damage.

If we are to live by the Rede and take the Law of Three seriously, these are things we need to be conscious of. Our entire lives must be guided by these basic principles. They should become a regular part of our outlook on the world, factoring into the decisions we make and the things we choose to do and not to do. When they are, we find our lives changing in remarkable ways.

GAIA'S EGG
A Story for Ostara

ABOUT OSTARA

The origins of Ostara, the spring equinox, are found in ancient celebrations of the Saxon goddess Eostre (also called Ostara). Not much has been written about Eostre herself, although she is sometimes said to have her origins in the great Canaanite goddess Astarte. In general, she is the Maiden aspect of the great Earth Mother who caused the lands to begin to flourish as the days grew warmer and the winter snows melted.

Whatever her origins, Eostre gave her name to the Christian celebration of Easter, which was clearly invented as a way to get early converts to move away from the Pagan celebration to a Christ-centered one. Christ's death and resurrection to bring life to his people is a classic image of the dying god causing the fields to flourish. The traditional Easter figure of the Easter bunny comes from the ancient Pagan reverence for the hare as a symbol of fertility. And the custom of coloring eggs for the holiday comes from the Pagan tradition of dyeing eggs—which were considered mysterious objects—scarlet to represent the sun.

The sun is of particular importance at Ostara. On this date, when the lengths of day and night are equal, the Goddess was said to give birth to the God in the form of the Child of Light, who was conceived at Yule and quickened in her belly at Imbolc. The sabbat itself is a celebration of the Earth's fertility and her ability to produce life.

In the Green Man tradition, Ostara is a time of giving birth to creativity. It is a ritual in which song, dance, music, and art of all kinds are used to celebrate the manifestation of the dreams and desires we have been nurturing during the winter.

Just as the Earth gives birth to the sun child, we give birth to the gifts of the spirit. It is a time for starting projects and beginning the workings that we will tend during the summer.

In this story, the name of Gaia, or Mother Earth, is used instead of Eostre. Since Eostre is simply the Maiden aspect of Mother Earth, they are essentially the same, although Gaia is a much more universal figure.

AS THE DAYS LENGTHENED and the strengthening sun warmed the Earth, the Green Man's heart grew full. The words he had been given in Brigid's house filled his head with their voices, and he found himself thinking often of what he had found in himself on that night when the fires lit the hilltops.

He watched as the first buds appeared on the trees and the purple and yellow crocuses pushed their heads from beneath the ground. On his windowsill sat the pot he received as a gift; the seeds he had planted on that magical eve had sprouted into tender green leaves that reached for the sun outside his window. He had tended his seeds carefully, and although he still did not know what they would become when fully grown, he knew that they would be beautiful.

Then, on the day when light and shadow were of equal length, the Green Man awoke and knew that it was time for him to go on a journey. He was surprised at his decision, since he had not been thinking about traveling anywhere and had no idea where he would go once he began. As he put the few things he would need into his pack, he sang the song of his heart and felt it pulling him into the warmth of the morning.

With his pack on his shoulder and his walking stick in his hand, the Green Man shut the door to his house and walked without thinking. He found himself going toward the river, which had recently shed its skin of ice and now flowed freely, its voice whispering of adventure as it splashed over the rocks on its way to he knew not where.

On the shore of the river, he discovered a small boat, brought by the river from its source somewhere in the hills of the Green Man's valley. Tethered to a tree, the boat had a prow carved with the face of a woman whose eyes called to the Green Man. He climbed into the boat and, taking the oars, launched himself into the current. The water reached for the boat and hurried it along on eager hands as the Green Man pushed himself clear of the rocks.

The river, swollen with melting snow, moved along swiftly. The Green Man watched as the banks rushed by, and it was all he could do to keep the boat from crashing against the stones that pushed up from the swirling water. But although the boat rose and fell in the arms of the river, he was not afraid. He felt the joy of the water beneath him and heard its song in his head.

The river ran through the valley, and after a time the Green Man was in unfamiliar country. He looked about him and saw that here the trees were greener, as if the sun above them shone more strongly than in his land. The grass was taller and from out of its tangled fingers rose bright flowers of yellow, red, and orange. He saw hares darting in the fields and in the waters around him otters raised their heads and looked at him with dark eyes before diving again.

The little boat rounded a bend and passed through a narrow opening between moss-covered rocks before the Green Man found himself floating on a vast lake that stretched as far as he could see. The lake was ringed by tall mountains, which held the dark water in their arms and hid the place from view. Above the water the sun hung round and glowing with fire, and its face was reflected in the gentle ripples that scattered across the lake's surface.

In the center of the lake was an island, rising green and inviting from the water, and it was toward this island that the Green Man rowed the boat. His arms were tired from pulling the oars, but the sun warmed him and the otters that splashed around him called him on, and after a time the boat reached the shallows around the island. The Green Man stepped from the boat into water that was clear and cool, and he pulled the boat behind him as he stepped onto the shore.

From his landing place there was a path leading away through the grass, and the Green Man followed it. It circled around the island in an ever-shrinking spiral, and he found himself walking as if through a labyrinth. As he went round and round, he was never quite able to see what lay at the center of the spiral, but he felt his heart quicken with each step. Around him he saw more of the hares that had watched him from the riverbanks. They darted in and out of view, their ears twitching as if listening to a voice he could not hear before they ran off again on some errands known only to themselves.

After circling the island seven times, each turn bringing him closer to the center, the Green Man found himself approaching a clearing. Before him the narrow path opened into a grove of birch trees, and he hurried to see what might be among them. Pushing through the thin screen of leaves, he stepped into a circle of green and gold light.

In the center of the grove was Gaia, sitting against a large boulder. Her bare skin glowed pink and golden against the moss that covered the ground, and her long hair flowed over her shoulders and breasts as sunshine over fields of flowers. She was great with child, and her hands rested on her belly. Around her were the hares the Green Man had seen in the spiral.

When she saw the Green Man standing before her, Gaia held out her hand. "It is time," she said. "The sun and moon are equal in the sky and spring is afoot. Come. Help me."

The Green Man dropped his pack and knelt beside Gaia. He took her hand in his. "What can I do for you?" he asked.

"I am going to give birth," she told him. "I need your help."

"But I know nothing of such things," the Green Man protested. "What can I do?"

"You can do more than you know," said Gaia. "Now watch. Kneel between my legs and be ready."

The Green Man knelt between Gaia's open legs. She placed his hands on her belly. Then she closed her eyes and began to sing a gentle song, a lullaby to a baby not yet in her arms. Beneath his hands, the Green Man felt something stir within her. Gaia's voice grew louder, and she pushed from deep within.

For a long time Gaia sang to her child. Her voice grew louder and louder, and the Green Man saw on her face both pain and joy. In his hands he felt the muscles of her body rippling, bringing out that which was within her. Above them, the sun continued to wait, watching and expectant, and around them the hares sat silently, noses twitching.

The Green Man did what he could to ease Gaia's work. He spoke softly to her. He rubbed his hands over her skin and wiped her face to cool her. He gave her water from his flask and fed her berries brought by the hares. For what seemed like many hours he watched and waited with her.

Then Gaia opened her throat and gave a cry of such force that the Green Man almost removed his hands from her belly to cover his ears. She threw her head back and pulled her knees to her chest. Her body shuddered, and from between her legs he saw something emerging into the light. He held out his hands as the goddess pushed again and delivered an enormous egg.

The Green Man looked at the egg in his hands. Beneath a film of Gaia's blood it shone with pale fire, like a newborn sun, and it was warm in his hands. He cleaned it with his shirt and held it up to Gaia, not understanding, and she smiled.

"Break it open," she told him. "See what is inside."

The Green Man held the egg in both hands and cracked the shell. The egg fell away into two halves, and the air was filled with a brightness that blinded the Green Man for a moment.

When he could see again, he looked into the egg and saw a child, golden as the sun that looked down on the grove. His hair was thick and shone like wheat, and his eyes were the color of amber. The child looked up at the Green Man and laughed, and it was as if summer had whispered in his ear.

Gaia reached out and took the child from the Green Man's grasp. She held him to her breast, and he began to drink of her milk.

"Thank you," she said. "You have served me well, and I will not forget."

"What is his name?" asked the Green Man, staring at the child in wonder.

"He is called Sol," said Gaia, "and you are his godfather. As he grows, so too shall you grow. His voice will call to you, and you will answer. You will create songs and stories for him. You will greet him each morning and sing him to sleep each evening. You will watch him grow, and he in turn will gift you with his radiance and warmth. Together, you will walk through the coming season and you will learn much from one another before it ends."

The Green Man looked down at the light child, who was now sleeping in his mother's arms. He found himself wanting to tell the child of his life, to share with him the many things he had thought about and learned since his visit to Brigid's house. And he knew that he would tell him of these things. He would tell him in songs, dances, and pictures. He would grow the story in his garden and he would bake it into the food he cooked.

"Now it is time to go," Gaia said to him. "Follow my hares. They will take you back again. But before you leave, take this and keep it with you."

Gaia held out an egg to the Green Man, and he took it from her.

"Inside is a word of power," she said. "Hold the egg in your hand and know that you hold a gift from me in thanks for what you have done here."

The Green Man put the egg into his pocket. He kissed Gaia gently and then the Child of Light. He stood, gathered his pack and stick, and walked out of the grove as Gaia began to sing to her child.

The hares led the Green Man back through the spiral, leaping and playing in celebration as they circled outward toward the edges of the island. But instead of coming once more to the shore of the lake, the Green Man found that the spiral path ended in the woods surrounding his valley. He was home once more, and when he looked behind him he saw only the tails of the hares disappearing into the trees as they raced back to their mistress.

The Green Man walked back to his home, and the sun shone on him as he passed through the fields. When he came to his house, he was surprised to see that the plants on his windowsill had bloomed in his absence into bright yellow sunflowers. Their full heads nodded to him from green stalks, and in their faces he saw the face of Sol, bright with wonder. Taking the plants into his garden, he planted them in a circle and watered them, knowing that in the coming weeks they, too, would grow into children of light who held their faces up to the sun.

As the day came to a close and the first sun of spring settled back into the mountains, the Green Man went inside. He took Gaia's egg from his pocket and held it in his hand. In his mind, he saw it covered in pictures. Taking his paints and brushes from the cupboard, he began to paint on the egg images that spoke to him of what might be inside. When he was finished, he set the egg in a place where he would see it often and be reminded of Gaia's gift and of the gifts that grew within him, waiting for him to bring them out into the sun.

Chapter 4

Exploring Deity

I have, since childhood, been fascinated by gods and goddesses. One of the first books I remember looking at with any serious interest was a beautifully illustrated version of the Bible for children. In particular, I recall an image of the burning bush out of which the voice of God spoke to Moses. I used to sit with the book in my lap, searching the orange and yellow flames, trying to see the face of God through them. I tried to imagine what the voice of God would sound like, what it would be like to hear it myself.

The other book that captivated me around this time was Ingri d'Aulaire and Edgar Parin d'Aulaire's delightful (and sadly now out-of-print) *Norse Gods and Giants*. Its brightly colored illustrations, so peculiar and yet so appealing, depicted the gods and goddesses of Scandinavian folklore engaged in all kinds of antics, and the accompanying stories were equally wonderful.

It's interesting now to think how equally affected I was by what could be considered opposing sides of a theological spectrum: Pagan and Christian, or sacred and the profane, if you will. The atmosphere in which I was raised was decidedly Christian, and it was made very clear to me, primarily through weekly attendance of Sunday school and church, that God (capital G) was the head honcho. Yet, somehow I wasn't willing to dismiss the Pagan gods so easily. I liked them, particularly when they made mistakes. The God of my mother's Bible never made mistakes, and frankly, that made me a little suspicious, like adults who always claimed to be right.

The more I read, the more goddesses and gods I met. The Greek and Roman deities joined the Norse in my extended family, although I confess I didn't find them nearly as interesting, given their perfect bodies, capricious personalities, and endless whining about the merest slights. Still, I was fond enough of them that I spent hours creating a diorama for an elementary school project that featured my G.I. Joe and *Star Trek* action figures dressed as Zeus and his gang.

As I grew older and read more about the various gods that existed outside the Christian world I was becoming ever more deeply involved in, I finally figured out what it was I liked about the other figures of other religions: They were a lot like me. They stumbled through life as best they could, and despite their divinity they frequently mucked things up. This, to me, was far more interesting than God and his squeaky-clean son. Jesus seemed like a nice enough fellow, but when the worst thing he did was kick around the stalls of some money changers, it was kind of hard to relate. I felt much more kinship with Loki, the Norse mischief maker who was constantly getting himself into one jam after another. And although God was mysterious and awe-inspiring (how could you not be impressed by someone who created the world or parted an entire sea), if I was picking sides for cosmic dodge ball I would have taken Odin or Zeus over him.

I felt slightly guilty about all of this. After all, I was reminded on a regular basis that God wasn't keen on being second fiddle to anyone, particularly not other gods. Whenever I spent time with my Norse and Greek friends, I did so with just the tiniest bit of worry that I'd eventually get zapped for it. It was okay to take the stories of these other gods as just that—myths and legends—but to consider them anything more was risking eternal hellfire.

Thinking about it now, I wonder what would happen if someone published an edition of the Bible subtitled "The Myths and Legends of the Christians." That's certainly how the Greek, Roman, and Norse stories were presented—are still most often presented. And this is one of the things that most fascinates me about Christian people, particularly the ones who look down on other religions as being collections of superstitions and fables. For if you take the elements of the Bible and look at them objectively, you've got some pretty weird stuff. Animals and humans created out of nothing. Plague and pestilence. Demons and angels. And then, of course, the whole sacrificial death and resurrection of Christ. This isn't exactly believable material. Yet, millions upon millions of people do believe it, and believe it with all of their heart and soul.

This, really, is the power of faith, the ability to believe in the face of all logic and reason. To be a Christian, you must believe the mythology, believe that the world was created by an omnipotent being who for a time interfered mightily in the affairs of humankind and then felt bad about it all and sent his son to be sacrificed for the continued sins of the world.

That's a pretty tall order, yet people all over the world do believe it. They base their entire lives on the belief that what the Bible portrays is true. Not myth. Not allegory. Truth. Imagine how deeply they must feel themselves affected by this faith if they can truly believe these things, truly believe in their hearts that these stories are worth basing their lives around.

This ability to believe isn't, of course, limited to followers of Christianity. Every faith has its own set of stories, its own set of gods and other spiritual beings who play a part in the theology of the faith. Every culture has its own stories about how the world came to be and about the supernatural beings who affect the lives of humankind.

So what about Wicca? What is its theology when it comes to deity? The easy answer would be to say that Wicca is a Goddess-oriented religion in which female deity is considered to hold a more elevated position than male deity. But this is too simplistic. For one thing, which goddess? Is there one Goddess of the Witches? No, there isn't. And do all Witches place female divinity above male divinity? No, they don't.

Some Witches don't involve themselves with deity at all. Some favor one goddess or god over the others. It's a matter of personal preference how a Witch expresses her or his spirituality when it comes to the goddesses and gods. There's no one Witch story about how the world came to be, or how the goddesses and gods have interacted with humankind. There is no established Witch mythology.

With no Bible, Koran, or Bhagavad Gita to base theology around, what do Witches do? The answer to this question is as individual as Witches themselves are. Witchcraft is unique in that within virtually every faith and culture that exists in the world there have been people who have been considered witches. Witchcraft, in effect, has often been seen as more of a worldview than as a specific spiritual path. This remains true today, which is why you have people like my friend the Jewitch, who considers herself equally Jewish and Witch.

What I personally find so powerful about Witchcraft is what I see as its fundamental ability to take the common thread that I feel runs through all the world's faiths and pull it out. Rather than focusing on the various dogmas and deities of religion, Witchcraft focuses on the *meaning* of spirituality. And when you do this, what you call your God or your Goddess, and what you believe about things like heaven and hell, sin and forgiveness, doesn't matter nearly as much.

There are some basic beliefs that, I think it is safe to say, most Witches would agree on. For one thing, Witches do not believe in the duality represented by God and Satan. There is no absolute evil or absolute good. And because there is no Satan, there is no hell or purgatory or any other place of torment reserved for those who "do wrong." Rather, there is personal responsibility to the world and to oneself. Personal happiness or unhappiness is not the result of a deity's approval or disapproval, but of the way in which you interact with the world and the way you choose to live your life.

With no heaven and hell, no God and Satan, what role does deity play in Witchcraft? My favorite Wiccan song, commonly used in Wiccan celebrations, contains the words, "We all come from the Goddess, and to her we shall return, like a drop of rain flowing to the ocean." For me, this sums up the whole of Wiccan thought. The Goddess is everything, because everything is connected and everything interacts with everything else. We are born out of nature and we return to it, perhaps to be born again, perhaps to be used in some other way to continue the never-ending cycle of growth and decay. None of us knows, really, what happens when we die, and so it's all speculation.

This Goddess, though, can take many different forms. She can be the African Oya, the temperamental mistress of the winds, or perhaps the Celtic Brigid, the contemplative goddess of fire and poetry. She can be the Hindu Kali, the goddess of destruction and rebirth, or the Norse Freya, the dazzling goddess of love and laughter. Traditionally, goddesses and gods were created to personify various aspects of nature or to explain things that otherwise could not be explained. The eruption of a volcano, for example, was attributed to the temper of the Hawaiian goddess Pele, while lightning was created by the wrath of Zeus as he raged in the heavens.

As I said, for Witches who do include deity in their spiritual practice, the options are virtually endless. How Witches view deity, too, is not always the same. Some may view the gods and goddesses as merely ways of personifying various forces, while some may believe that these entities actually exist in some way. There is no right or wrong way to view things in Wicca, no one belief all Witches hold to be true when it comes to deity.

As a child, I was taught that God existed. He was a real being of some kind who was able to manifest himself physically and to physically alter the natural world. I was taught that if I wanted something, I could pray to God and talk directly to him. I believed that he was up there, somewhere, watching over me in a very real way.

How do I view deity now? I would love to discover someday that the gods and goddesses exist bodily. I would love to encounter one of them on the street or in a forest. I like to think that at one time they really did walk the earth, having adventures and interacting with the rest of us. To know that the myths and legends are really true would be extraordinary.

In reality, I see the gods and goddesses as attempts to put human faces on ideas that are difficult to conceptualize. Even more important, I see them as ways in which we take parts of ourselves and magnify them to a point where they take on cosmic significance. By doing this, we allow ourselves to become players in a game that spans eternity and has meaning beyond what we might see as our ordinary, unimportant lives.

Take, for a moment, the whole world of superheroes. Why are characters such as Batman and Wonder Woman so appealing? Why do we dress up as Superman or the Green Lantern on

Halloween? We do it because these characters are in many ways like us but with something extra that makes them special. The most popular superheroes don't originate outside of humanity, they come from within it. Peter Parker is bitten by a radioactive spider and becomes Spiderman. Policeman Jim Corrigan is murdered by his enemies and is reborn as the Spectre. Regular people like us find themselves with extraordinary powers.

In many cultures, it is the same with the gods and goddesses. The orishas of Africa, and the related voodoo religion of Haiti and the Americas, for example, are populated with divine entities who act and behave like human beings (some of whom even began their existence as human beings and became gods or goddesses). We, as people, have a difficult time relating to all-powerful beings. We like our gods to be more like we are, hence the enormous popularity among the Hindu community of television programs and comic books about the monkey god Hanuman and his adventures, or the Norse and Greek myths that captured my attention as a child. Even Christianity, with its untouchable, unseeable God, provides a much-needed dose of humanity in the form of Jesus Christ.

This is how I see the various goddesses and gods I involve in my own spiritual practices. They are symbols, beings who embody certain characteristics or talents that I find useful to my own work. Really, these are my own qualities and traits magnified many times over. By focusing these qualities onto the goddesses and gods, I empower myself by allowing what might seem (to me) my insufficient strength in a particular area to be increased.

Think about prayer for a moment. When a person prays to a god for help, what is she really doing? Is she asking a divine being to intercede on her behalf, to accomplish something she can't do herself? Perhaps. Certainly, there are many people who believe that is exactly what prayer is. But this view assumes that the entity being prayed to exists and can, in fact, manipulate the physical world.

What if, however, the petitioner sees the god being prayed to as an extension of herself, extension that, for her, embodies characteristics of herself that, in her present circumstances, don't seem adequate enough to overcome the problem at hand. By calling on this god, by focusing her energies and intentions on that embodiment, maybe she can increase her trust in her own abilities and bring about the outcome she requires.

That's how I see the goddesses and gods of my faith. For example, if I feel the need to do some work around the issue of getting out of a stagnant period in my life, my thoughts turn to goddesses such as Oya or Kali. Both goddesses are considered mistresses of change, destroying the old so that something new can take root. If I'm feeling stuck in my life, it helps me to connect in various ways (which we'll discuss later, I promise) with these deities because it helps me focus my mind on achieving what they represent to me. Do I think that somewhere out in the cosmos Kali and Oya are sitting, listening to me talk to them? That would be excellent, wouldn't it? But I suspect they would have better things to do.

No, what I think happens is that by focusing my thoughts on the aspects of these goddesses that relate to my situation, I realize those aspects in myself and make change happen. Similarly, if I'm feeling overwhelmed by anger, I might take time to sit and focus my attention on a goddess such as Kuan Yin, the Buddhist embodiment of compassion and peace. Again, I don't believe that because I call on her Kuan Yin bends down and taps me with her celestial wand, making my anger vanish. I think that by connecting with feelings of peace as they are embodied in Kuan Yin I awaken them in myself.

In short, the goddesses and gods of Witchcraft are, to me,

tools to reach within myself. This isn't to say that I don't respect them as entities. I do. I think that anything created by our minds and repeatedly recognized as having importance to us spiritually takes on enormous power. But do I think the gods play games with my life? No, I do not. Do I think that they are beings I can call on at my whim? Again, no.

Traditionally, Wicca has focused on goddess figures. *The* Goddess, really, is any goddess. She is the embodiment of nature and its cycles, both light and dark, life and death. Which face she wears depends on which name you attach to her. But all goddesses are part of the one, each simply a different face with a different name.

I see the gods the same way, of course. Each one represents a different part of me, a different aspect of who I am as a human being. Apollo is the cool thinker, the Hindu elephant-headed god Ganesha is the happy remover of obstacles, and the orisha Obatala is the ever-present wise father figure. Again, each god embodies a mood or strength from which, depending on the situation, I draw strength, comfort, or joy.

Green Man spirituality differs from traditional Wicca in that, although goddesses are very much a part of our practices, the Path of the Green Man is centered around a God (of the big G variety) figure. The Green Man name has two origins. The first is general, a green man (lowercase g and m) is someone who lives in harmony with nature. The second comes from the actual Green Man, a figure in British folklore who has a face made of leaves. He is the embodiment of the forest and of wild magic, a creature born from the trees and plants and devoted to protecting them.

The Green Man can be seen as a deity in and of himself, but really he is the practitioner of Green Man Wicca, and not the primary focus. That role belongs to Cernunos. Cernunos (also spelled Cernnunos, Kernunnos, and various other ways) is a

Celtic god of the woods. His name means, literally, "Horned One," and he is most often depicted with the antlers of a stag. Considered a shaman, he is a mysterious figure about whom little lore exists apart from the fact that he was considered the lord of the wood.

Cernunos is the god associated with Green Man Wicca. He is the Horned God met by the Green Man when he begins his journey on the path. He is the protector of nature who has much to teach us. To me, the Green Man acts as his student and servant, seeking to understand the wisdom the Horned One has and to live his life in harmony with the natural world as Cernunos does. I see him as a figure who represents what I want to achieve in my life and who possesses qualities I wish to see strengthened in my life. Visualizing him as the Horned God helps me do this, as it gives me something on which to focus my thoughts and around which to build a system of expressing my beliefs. Although I would love to discover that the Horned God resides somewhere in a forest clearing, waiting for me to find my way to him, I see him more as someone I want to be, my inner strengths brought together and made whole.

While we're talking about Cernunos, I want to make a tiny detour and discuss a common misconception about Pagan spirituality. People often view Pagan spirituality and Christian spirituality as completely opposite sides of a spiritual coin. Pagan beliefs are the "old ways," and Christianity is the "new way." The implication, of course, is that a lot of uneducated people were bumbling around worshiping stars, rocks, and trees until Christianity came along and set everyone straight. Indeed, in d'Aulaire and d'Aulaire's *Norse Gods and Giants* book I loved so much, the story ends with the Norse gods being defeated by Christianity, a climax that never failed to leave me angry.

Cernunos is a perfect example of this. With his horns and wild nature, Cernunos represented everything the newly minted

Christians saw as threatening. It doesn't take a lot of imagination to see how the Horned One of the Celtic woods was transformed into the Devil of Christianity, his earthiness turned to evilness, his love of life to carnal lusts. And so it was for much of Pagan spirituality. We'll talk more about this in later chapters, but for now it's important to note that many of what are erroneously believed to be Christian-created holidays and holy days are in fact Pagan celebrations that had the non-Christian hearts removed from them. Easter, which was briefly discussed in the previous chapter, is a variation on a Germanic celebration of the goddess Eostre, an agricultural and fertility goddess who was symbolized by hares (didn't you ever wonder why we have the Easter Bunny?).

Similarly, many of the Pagan gods and goddesses were appropriated by Christianity and changed into less-offensive forms to make them acceptable (e.g., the Celtic goddess Brigid equated with Mary) or more beastly (e.g., Cernunos becoming Satan) to render them unholy. Interestingly, this hiding of deity behind new masks was reversed years later during the time of slavery when followers of certain African religions, threatened with punishment if they were caught practicing their faith, put the names of Catholic saints over their traditional gods and goddesses and went right on practicing beneath the noses of their clueless masters.

Part of my fondness for Cernunos is the fact that his reputation was spoiled so badly by Christianization. More than that, though, is the simple fact that he represents what I want to achieve with my spirituality. And that's how you should choose the gods and goddesses you work with (if you decide to work with any). They should mean something to you personally.

This leads us to the topic of "gay" gods and goddesses. Frequently, when I discuss Wiccan spirituality with other gay people, they want to know who the gay gods are. I understand this desire. We like to think that there are deities who are "ours." We want to relate to them, and what more intimate way could we relate to them than if we share a similar sexuality. After all, don't Catholic monks maintain a vow of celibacy because they believe Christ did?

The truth is, I don't know of any specifically gay gods or goddesses. Often, gay men will choose to honor gods such as Apollo, who was known for his beauty and his fondness for handsome young men, or the lusty forest god Pan, who is often portrayed as a well-endowed fellow devoted to music and lovemaking. Then, of course, there's Hermaphrodite, the offspring of Hermes and Aphrodite who possessed both a male and female spirit. But by and large, there aren't a lot of queer gods running around.

Really, though, it doesn't matter. With some notable exceptions, who slept with whom was not generally of terrible importance to the stories of the gods. And given the sexual tendencies of the cultures with the most well-developed mythologies, they probably assumed the gods were just as adventurous as they were when it came to their romantic lives. Occasionally, romantic dalliances do play integral parts in spiritual mythologies (particularly in the African orisha religion, where certain goddesses had long-standing feuds over some of the gods) but again, it's the character of a particular goddess or god that is really important.

I understand the desire for a "gay religion," so to speak, but I think focusing on whether a goddess or god might be considered to be on our team romantically is to miss the point. Our sexuality, while important, is not what defines us as human beings, so to base a theology on that is a mistake. The Catholic insistence on celibacy for priests, and the tragic results of this, are a perfect example of how fixation on one aspect of life to the exclusion of others can result in spiritual disaster.

Rather than focus on which god or goddess best represents our sexuality, we need to look at what aspects of our overall lives are represented in the deities we choose to honor. Not that sexuality doesn't come into things. More than one Christian saint wrote ecstatically about experiencing God in ways that rival the steamiest romance novel. And I find Cernunos, for example, to be an extremely sexy figure. But I'm not going to bed with him; I'm looking to him as an example of what I would like my life to be.

So as gay men attempting to develop a spiritual path or tradition, we need to select for ourselves gods and goddesses we relate to. How do we do this? There are different ways of thinking about this. Some people believe that it's best to stick with deities who emanate from your own cultural background. The idea is that you already have something in common with these gods and goddesses by virtue of your heritage and that connecting with them will be made easier by this. If, for example, you happen to come from a Celtic background, you would then incorporate the Celtic gods into your practice.

I think that's a fine approach if it works for you. For me, that would be like eating the same food all the time simply because it's the food of your heritage. Since I come from Irish and Norwegian background, I can assure you that eating the food of my people every day is not a prospect I look forward to happily. Nor do I wish to confine myself—as much as I love them— to the gods and goddesses of my ancestors. True, I find that I connect easily with many of the Norse deities, but that probably has as much to do with my positive introduction to them as a child as it does with the fact that my maternal grandmother's family came from a small town outside of Oslo.

Personally, I find it very exciting to discover gods and goddesses from different cultures and see how they can be worked into my spiritual journey. For example, I am extremely devoted to the Hindu goddess Kali. Apart from a trip to India a few years ago, I have no particular cultural connection to India. But Kali speaks to me in an intensely personal way, and I find myself returning to her again and again in my work.

Sometimes, too, different deities will make themselves known to you unexpectedly. Some years ago I arranged a telephone consultation with Philip John Neimark, the author of *The Way of the Orisa* and one of America's leading teachers in the orisha religion. I'd recently been studying African spirituality and had asked Philip if he could determine who my guardian orisha (spirit) was.

Philip had never spoken to me before and knew nothing whatsoever about me. I listened as he went through the ritual on his end of the phone. After a minute or two he paused and said, "This is very unusual."

These are words you seldom want to hear from either your doctor or an orisha priest. As I waited anxiously, Philip told me that according to his reading my guardian was Orisha Oko, one of the lesser known of the spirits and a fairly rare one to have as a guardian. "Did you ever have an experience with a snake?" he asked.

As it happens, I have. I was born in Africa, where my family lived for several years during my childhood. One afternoon when I was probably a year or two old, my father walked out of our house to discover me sitting in a sandbox "playing" with a cobra. According to family legend, I was talking to the snake as it sat looking at me. I have no recollection of this event whatsoever, but the story of how my father grabbed me and ran into the garage, with the snake chasing him, was told repeatedly when I was younger.

I told Philip this story and he laughed. "That explains it," he said. "Orisha Oko takes the form of a cobra when he wants to talk to you. He was simply introducing himself."

I may be symbolically African by accident of birth, but certainly not by heritage. Yet, I do find myself deeply interested in African religion, and once I learned of Orisha Oko's existence, I began to incorporate him into my practice. He became another window through which to see who I am and what my place in the world is.

As you begin your own practice, explore the world's pantheons and look for deities who speak to you. Sometimes the connection will be obvious, but other times you may find yourself attracted to a god or goddess for reasons you can't immediately identify. That's okay. Develop a relationship with that deity. Read about her. Discover stories about him. Look for things you have in common, traits of hers you wish you had more of, or ideals he embodies that you want to manifest in yourself. A huge part of Witchcraft, particularly the Path of the Green Man, is about exploration. In fact, as you read the stories that make up the "Journey of the Green Man" cycle, you will see that the Green Man encounters different figures from different traditions, all of whom work to help him along the way.

Exercise: Finding the God or Goddess Within You

What exactly *are* the goddesses and gods of Wicca? That's open to interpretation. Some people believe that the various deities really exist. Other people think of them as each representing a different aspect of one main deity. And still others see the goddesses and gods not as real entities but as symbolic representations of different aspects of *our* personalities.

How you see the different goddesses and gods is up to you. But however you see them, it can be very informative and fun to research the different deities that you feel drawn to. Why?

Because each one of us has special qualities, skills, and challenges to face that make us the unique people we are. By getting closer to these aspects of ourselves, we can better understand who we are and what we can do with our talents. One way we can do this is by learning more about goddesses and gods who share those talents.

Finding the god or goddess within you is just a fun way of learning about different deities and finding one or more of them you relate to. How do you do this? First, you read everything you can find about different gods and goddesses. There are many, many books available about the deities of different traditions. Go to your library or a bookstore and look through some of them. Don't worry about doing it "right." This isn't an assignment. You're just going to read the stories of the gods and goddesses. If you already have an interest in a particular culture—say the ancient Celts or the Yoruba tribes of Africa— read more about it. If you don't know much about gods and goddesses at all, look through different kinds of books and see what you are drawn to. Part of magic is opening yourself up to possibilities, and if you approach learning about the gods and goddesses with an open mind and heart, you'll find yourself being taken in surprising directions.

As you read, note any deities you find particularly interesting. Don't worry if the deities you're attracted to are your gender or not. It doesn't matter. A man can feel kinship with the Greek goddess Athena, just as a woman can find a lot she relates to in the story of the Norse god Odin. Nor do you have to pick a goddess or god who is just like you. It's the story and the qualities of the deity you're interested in. You may find the fearsome Russian witch Baba Yaga fascinating, even if you're not at all like her yourself, or you might like the wonderful story of the Hindu monkey god Hanuman despite not knowing anything about Hinduism. The important thing is to read as much as you can, find one or more godesses and gods you want to know more about, and start from there.

Once you find a deity you would like to work with more closely, find out all you can about her or him. Make a list of the characteristics you relate to in the goddess or god, as well as the characteristics the deity has that you wish *you* had. For example, maybe you find yourself drawn to the African goddess Oya, who is known for her fierce determination and independent spirit. Perhaps you wish you were more like Oya. Write down how you would like to be more like her. Or maybe you relate to the Celtic god Cernunos, the central figure in Green Man Wicca, because you, too, like to spend time in nature. Write down the characteristics you share with Cernunos. Putting these things in writing will help you understand more deeply why you feel drawn to the deity you choose.

What you do now is up to you. Perhaps you simply want to draw or find a picture of your chosen deity and put it somewhere where you see it and are reminded of your connection. Or maybe you want to do more. If you would like to do a simple ritual designed to connect you with your chosen deity, you can do something like the following.

Decorate an altar with images or symbols of the particular deity you wish to work with. An altar can be any place where you can set up an area devoted to your deity. For years I used a small telephone table with the legs cut down. Your altar can be as simple or as elaborate as you like, from a corner of your desk to a large shrine taking up a whole room.

Whatever your version of an altar is, decorate it in a way that celebrates the qualities of the deity you've chosen. This might mean using candles in a color associated with your goddess or god, finding objects that represent her or him, or getting flowers associated with the deity. For example, when invoking the goddess Freya, you might decorate your altar with pink and white candles (Freya's favorite colors) and roses (her favorite flower). Similarly, you could use blue candles for the water god Poseidon, or red flowers for the goddess Kali. Use your imagination and make your altar as magical as you can. The one thing you will need for this exercise is a candle to represent the goddess or god you're working with.

Sit in front of your altar and think about the deity you want to know better. When you are ready, call to the goddess or god. You don't have to use any fancy words or anything. Just talk to the goddess or god. Introduce yourself as if you're meeting someone at a party. Tell her or him what you hope to accomplish and describe why you have asked him or her to be with you. Nothing strange is going to happen here. You won't hear voices or see anything weird. Just imagine yourself talking to the deity you want to work with. And you don't have to say the words out loud if you don't want to. You can say them silently. The important thing is to feel like you're really talking to the goddess or god.

When you feel that you have said what you need to say, light the candle you have chosen to represent the deity. Tell her or him that by lighting the candle, you are entering into an agreement. For the duration of your work (perhaps from one full moon to the next, for a week, or however long you want) you will work together. Tell the goddess or god that you will take to heart any lessons she or he may have for you. Ask that in return the deity share with you the gifts she or he possesses that you think will aid you. For example, if you have chosen to work with the goddess Brigid because she is believed to inspire artists, ask her to lend you her gift of artistic inspiration. Be specific about what you want. And if you don't have any specific wants, just tell the deity that you would like to learn whatever she or he has to teach you.

Once you have asked the goddess or god to work with you,

sit and watch the candle flame for some time. Think about the deity you have just called and about the work you will do together. You might take the time to actually write down your goals for the work. This gives you something to compare your actual progress against later.

Throughout the moon cycle or period you work with your chosen goddess or god, light your candle and think about the agreement you've made. Also remember to thank her or him periodically, and remember to write down what happens to you in a journal. Things that might seem insignificant at first may turn out to be hugely important in a larger picture. It is fascinating to see how the different deities work once you ask them into your life.

At the end of your moon cycle or chosen period, decorate your altar once more and thank your chosen deity for working with you. This doesn't mean that she or he still won't be part of your life; it's just a good way to officially end the magic you've been doing. You may then decide to work with another deity and see what she or he has to show you. The goddesses and gods—whether you see them as actual entities or as symbols—represent many different aspects of life. By working with them, and by learning how you are like them, you will discover the goddess or god within yourself.

THE KISS OF PAN

A Story for Beltane

———— ∞ ————

ABOUT BELTANE

In the Celtic tradition, Beltane is the beginning of summer. The name means "Bel-fire," referring to a fire lit in honor of a prototypical Celtic solar/fire deity, one of whose names was Bel.

Traditionally, Beltane, or May Eve, celebrations did not officially begin until the High King of Ireland lit the first fire on Tara Hill, the seat of the kingdom. Once this first fire was lit, fires were lit all across the country. People then jumped over the fire to bring themselves lovers and ensure pregnancy, and cattle and other livestock were driven through the ashes of Beltane fires or between two fires to ensure their safety and productivity.

In a similar way, it was very common for Pagans to spend Beltane Eve making love in the fields. By doing so, they both celebrated the abundance provided by the gods and also gave back to the earth an offering designed to ensure continuing fertility for all concerned. Often, these couplings were random, with the participants choosing one another regardless of their own marital or relationship status. The idea was to celebrate pleasure, not fidelity, and many children conceived on May Eve bore remarkable resemblance to men who were not their mothers' lawful husbands.

Another traditional Beltane symbol is the maypole, around which celebrants would dance holding ribbons, weaving in and out in a pattern until the pole was tightly wrapped with color. Again, the symbolism is obvious. The phallic maypole, offered up in gaily colored ribbons, was a gift to the gods of prosperity. Plus, it was a lot of fun.

In this story, the Green Man partakes of these Beltane pleasures in his own—queer—way. Only here it is Pan, the patron god of many a gay man, who initiates him into the joys of May Eve. I chose Pan for his connection to the woods and fields and also for his devotion to gay male sexuality and its wonders. He is the Earth Father who calls us to come together on his altar. He serenades us with his flute and arouses us with his touch. He is unbridled joy and unashamed pleasure. In meeting him, the Green Man discovers that sometimes accepting these things is its own magic, a magic deep and old as the woods themselves.

While this story is about fertility, it is fertility of spirit that is celebrated, the fertility of men joining with men to give thanks for what Pan and the other gods have given us.

AS SPRING GREW to fullness and the Green Man's circle of sunflowers climbed up toward the light, so did his heart fill with joy. During the day, he walked the fields blooming with flowers and rejoiced in their colors, and sometimes when the sun was at its highest he lay in the swaying grasses and felt the warmth of the earth beneath him. In his bed at night, he watched the moon outside his window and heard the sounds of forest creatures calling to one another on the wind that rustled the leaves. Sometimes their voices filled him with longing, and then he would run his hands over his body and dream of holding another close to him. Everywhere the world was bursting with creation, and in the Green Man the power waited to be freed.

One night when the longing was especially strong and the Green Man tossed in his bed as he dreamt of love and the night beasts sang in the shadows, the moon rose full and golden over the world. Its light shined on the Green Man and he sat up. Rubbing the sleep from his eyes, he went to the window and looked out.

Beneath him, some distance off in the field, there was a fire. At first, the Green Man feared that somehow a spark had caused the grass to burn. But the fire, while large, was not burning wild. It had been lit with purpose.

Curious, the Green Man ran out into the night, forgetting even to put on his clothes. The air was gentle and heavy with heat, and as he ran out into the field his blood rose and sweat beaded his skin. Shortly he arrived at the fire, and found that it was even larger than he'd first thought.

Holding his hand against his eyes, he looked toward the flames and saw that beyond them rose a tall pole like a leafless tree. Figures moved around the place where the fire was, darting in and out of his view. They were strange figures, leaping and holding their hands up to the heavens. Some seemed to be horned, and the Green Man wondered if perhaps he had stumbled across one of the secret rites held by the creatures he knew sometimes emerged from their homes deep in the forests to dance under the moon. The sound of laughter floated up from the flames, and the notes of a flute danced in the air like fireflies.

"Who is there?" called the Green Man boldy. "Who has made this fire in my field?"

The voices ceased, and the music faded. Around the fire, the shadows stood still and the air was quiet save for the crackling of the logs.

"Who is there?" the Green Man called once more. Already he missed the sound of the flute and the happy laughter.

For long minutes there was silence. Then out of the shadows stepped a man. He, too, was naked, and his body glowed in the light as he came forward and held out his hand.

"Come," he said. "Come and dance."

"Who are you?" asked the Green Man, seeing the small horns that rose from the man's brow.

The man laughed, sensing the Green Man's wonder. "I attend the bearded one," he said, his eyes bright. "I dance for him and welcome him on this, his night."

"Who is he?" said the Green Man. "This master of yours. Is he here?"

"He is all about us," said the man, sweeping his hand in a circle that took in the night and everything in it. "It is his music you hear. It is his song we sing, and his song that moves us. Come and join us."

The horned man took the Green Man's hand and led him forward past the firelight to where the great pole rose up from the earth. Then he saw that all about the pole were other men, their hair damp with sweat and their bodies rinsed in the warmth of the night. Some wore leaves and flowers in their hair. Others held drums and sticks in their hands. Some were horned, while others looked like any of the many men who farmed the countryside in the towns that lay beyond the Green Man's valley.

The Green Man looked about him for the bearded one the horned man had spoken of, but saw none who truly fit that name. Then the music began again, the flute piping a tune that made the Green Man ache to dance. The drummers joined the song, beating in time as they stamped their feet. All around the pole men took up the ends of ribbons that were attached to the top and began to move in a circle about the pole, some moving in one direction and some in the other.

One by one they sang, adding their voices to the swelling music as they started to weave in and out, moving under the upheld arms of their neighbors and then lifting their own arms for the next man to pass beneath. As they danced, the ribbons wove themselves tightly about the pole. There was no tune that the Green Man could follow, yet the sound they made lulled him into a trance as he moved with them, strong hands on either side guiding him. As he danced among the others, he looked into their eyes and knew that he was among brothers.

The Green Man had no idea how long he danced under the moon with the strange men. He heard only their low voices rising up into the night to serenade the moon, felt only their bodies around him as they swayed and stamped, circled and returned, wrapping the great pole in ribbons. The fire grew stronger as they danced, brighter and more alive. He felt his blood moving with theirs, and it seemed to him that his skin was touched by many hands.

And then, just as the ribbon ran out and fell from his fingers and he thought his head would burst open from the beating of the drums in his heart and the fire in his belly, he heard a voice call out, "Go now! Go into the fields together."

All around the Green Man his brothers dropped their ribbons, set down their drums, and moved away into the night in pairs and in groups. Some held hands and leapt over the fire, shouting with joy before tumbling into the darkness. Others moved silently into the shadows as if sinking into water. He watched as the figures slipped into the grass, some kneeling on the ground among the flowers and others falling into one another's arms. He heard the sounds like those of the night creatures, rich with lust, and he shivered.

Then the Green Man felt a hand on his shoulder and heard a voice command him to follow. He turned and saw walking away from him a figure gilded in moonlight, his naked back pale as marble as he passed through the men already lying entangled in the tall grass and in one another. Without thought, he followed the man into the fields, walking until they came to a place where a large oak tree thrust up from the earth and spread its arms out wide above them.

The man turned and looked into the Green Man's face. In the moment before their bodies entwined, the Green Man saw in the other's eyes the deepest shadows of the woods. He saw the horns on his head, larger than those of the others, and saw, too, that his chin was bearded like that of a he-goat. Then he felt the man's mouth on his, his tongue against his, and he was lowered into the grass by strong arms.

The Green Man's skin burned as the bearded one's fingers traced the valleys and peaks of his body. He gasped as a warm mouth closed over a nipple and knowing fingers worked him to hardness. He pushed himself against the embracing hands and felt the earth beneath him with every muscle. This was what he dreamed of alone in his bed, and his heart and body opened to it as to a cooling rain.

As the horned one moved down his body, the Green Man ran his hands over the broad shoulders and around the strong neck until his fingers entwined in the man's hair. He pushed his head downward, feeling the warmth of the man's tongue as it licked at his skin. It had been a long time since the Green Man had lain with another, and although he was used to the feel of his own hands on his body, the man's touch filled him with a longing he thought he had forgotten.

The bearded man's mouth closed over the Green Man's cock, drawing him into a pool of warmth. He slid deep into the man's throat, and a groan escaped his own lips, joining those that floated like night moths on the air around him as the other men, too, coupled in the fields.

As the bearded man played along the length of the Green Man, one of his hands moved down and the Green Man felt a finger slip inside of him. Slowly it moved in and out in time with the man's strokes, teasing the Green Man and hinting at more. He felt himself rising up to meet the bearded man's mouth and trying to draw more of his hand inside of himself. His whole body cried out to become one with the other man's.

The horned man knelt in the grass and slid his strong arms beneath the Green Man's legs, drawing them up against his shoulders. Behind him the fire still burned, and his shadow rose up against the moon. The Green Man looked at the muscled lines of body above him, saw the shadow of the man's smile just before he pushed forward, and then his breath left him as it was replaced by pleasure.

The bearded man moved in and out of the Green Man with a motion like the wind parting the grass. The Green Man felt him deep inside and his head was filled with thoughts of the sun warming his skin as he walked the fields, of the embrace of the cool water when he leapt naked into the river to swim. He remembered long afternoons spent working in his garden when the dirt covered his hands and face and the sweat painted it into patterns on his chest. With each thrust of his hips, the horned man caused another memory to rise up and fill the Green Man's head with joy.

As they moved together, the bearded man leaned forward, pressing his body against the Green Man's so that their skin met. Still, he filled the Green Man, and the heat between them was thick and dizzying.

"It is not every man who meets me here," said the soft voice. "You were called tonight, this night when men celebrate my gifts."

"Who are you?" asked the Green Man, his fingers touching the man's face, sliding over the rough horns and parted lips.

"I am called many things," the man said. "I am master of the wood and field. The keeper of the wild things and their secrets. The grapes grow to give me wine, and the corn to make my bread. The birds sing for me and the beasts sport for my amusement."

"And what of me?" asked the Green Man. "How do I serve you?"

"I am ever-living," the horned one said. "The soil of the forest is my blood, and the rain my sweat. But there is much of man in me, and you remind me of that. Whenever you love in my fields or dance beneath the stars that light my house, you make me strong. And you make yourselves strong."

The Green Man felt himself growing close. The scent of the bearded one surrounded him, the smell of leaves, thunderstorms, and ripe fruit. The air was heavy, and his blood made his skin flush with heat and expectation.

"Joy is my song," the man whispered as he brought the

Green Man nearer and nearer. "Sing it often. It feeds the earth and makes it rich. Do not fear pleasure, but enjoy it abundantly."

The Green Man felt himself spill over, and called out as his body shook with release. He felt the bearded one stiffen inside him, and a rush of heat flooded his depths as if a summer rain had broken. Around them, the night shimmered as their cries joined the many others filling the darkness.

Afterward, the Green Man lay in the bearded one's arms in the grass, feeling his heart beat. He knew that all around them men were doing the same, their hands and mouths exploring one another as the fire burned and time stood still. He knew that the land had drunk deeply of their love, and that the fields would be rich because of it. He also knew that their souls had drunk deeply of the same passion and that it would fuel them for many nights to come. And thinking these things, he closed his eyes and slept.

When he awoke, it was morning and the sun was looking down at him where he slept. The men were gone from the field, and there was no sign of the fire from the evening past, nor of the pole around which they had danced. The Green Man stretched himself in the grass and discovered that where he and the horned one had lain the ground was covered in dark purple flowers. Their scent was that of fermenting grapes and decaying wood, the smell of earth returning to itself that which it had created. The Green Man drank deeply of the flowers, and remembered once more the touch of the bearded one, both within and without him. He felt himself begin to harden, and as the sun warmed his skin he gripped himself lovingly, closed his eyes, and offered to the god of the fields a celebration of the pleasures of men.

Chapter 5

Exploring Magic

In Susanna Clarke's delightful novel *Jonathan Strange and Mr. Norrell*, a wild, enchanting look at what the world of nineteenth-century England might have been like had magic and magicians been part of everyday society, the magician Mr. Norrell is asked by a gentleman what one needs to work magic. He replies, "I will tell you a little trick, my lord, the more apparatus a magician carries about with him—coloured powders, stuffed cats, magical hats and so forth—the greater fraud you will eventually discover him to be!"

Like the word *witch*, the word *magic* is surrounded by all kinds of fanciful notions and misconceptions. Images of Harry Potter and his would-be sorcerer friends pointing their wands and mumbling secret words come to mind. Or perhaps we envision *Macbeth*'s three witches standing over their bubbling cauldron, working mischief and cackling in delight. Popular culture depicts magic in many different ways, but it is always dramatic and exciting, filled with grand enchantments, secret spells, and the harnessing of some unknown power.

This is not at all surprising. Magic is supposed to be mysterious, something unexplainable and awe-inspiring. Even the most mundane of magicians should be able to produce illusions and perform tricks that, on the surface, defy science, logic, and the laws of nature, such as sawing someone in two or producing a rabbit out of a supposedly empty top hat. As for witches, well, we expect them to be capable of all manner of arcane activities.

Go to any shop catering to Witchcraft, or to any gathering devoted to Wiccan spirituality, and you're guaranteed to find a range of items supposedly devoted to magical purposes. Potions, powders, candles, amulets, incense, tools, clothing, herbs, crystals, oils—the list of magical accoutrements is positively endless. Similarly, bookshelves are lined with volumes promising to reveal spells for love, money, success, health, and so on and so on. Magic is big business, and there are a great many people lined up both to buy and to sell.

Like Mr. Norrell, I will let you in on a little secret: You don't need any of these things to do magic. All you need is your mind.

Oh, sure, you can dress up in robes and light candles and make potions if you want to. There's nothing at all wrong with these things, and they can be a lot of fun to do. But there's no magic in them, not really. That all comes from within you. Everything else is merely props that help you get the job done.

So if finding just the right herb or selecting just the right colored candle isn't going to make magic work, what's it all about? The best definition I've ever heard of magic came from the writer Dion Fortune, who said that magic is the art of changing consciousness at will.

This isn't quite as sexy as the idea of mixing ingredients for a spell, is it? In fact, it sounds a lot like psychology. And that's exactly what it is. The human mind is an absolutely amazing thing, capable of things we are only beginning to understand. Memory, for example, is probably the most "magical" thing I can think of. How do we store images, thoughts, sounds, and feelings? How does a collection of fairly simple cells accomplish this? Science has only partially explained the intricate workings of the brain. There's so much more to discover, and every day we learn more about how powerful our minds are.

Magic comes from within us and harnesses this incredible store of power found within our minds. To build on Fortune's definition, I would say that magic is the practice of using our innate abilities to make changes in our lives and in the world. There are many different tools we can use to help us do this, but basically this is what magic is.

This true definition of magic may not be as thrilling as the notion of waving a wand and turning someone into a toad, but in practice it's much more satisfying. Learning how to look within yourself and use the qualities you possess to transform your life is one of the most rewarding things you will ever do. Seeing the difference you can make in your life, and by extension in the world, will empower you more than any fictional spell ever could.

Before you go throwing away those books of spells you might already have purchased, wait a moment. They aren't useless by any means. It's how you approach them that makes the difference. Take, for example, the ever-popular love spell. There are literally thousands and thousands of different spells that promise to bring love into your life. Do they really work?

A friend of mine, when he first began to study Witchcraft, decided to perform one of these love spells. Specifically, he wanted to meet someone who resembled a particular porn star with whom he was infatuated, an improbable likelihood for many reasons. But my friend was determined. He located a love spell and performed it, envisioning this man he found so sexually exciting, and even incorporating a photograph from a porn magazine into his spell ritual.

A few days later (and I am not making this up) he met, at a party, a fellow who was visiting friends in town and who could have been the identical twin of his porn star fantasy man. The two hit it off, and soon found themselves in bed. My friend enjoyed several days of sexual bliss with his paramour, and when it was over he was quite pleased with how his attempt at working magic had turned out. At least until a week later, when he discovered that his fantasy man had left him with a very real sexually transmitted disease.

Now, there are several ways to look at this story. You could say that my friend had no business doing something like a love spell and that the STD he picked up (and got rid of after a couple of painful months) was some kind of punishment for dabbling in things he didn't understand. The more useful way to see it is that my friend accomplished what he set out to do, but that perhaps his intentions were not exactly what they should have been.

Intention is an often-used word in discussions of magic. Intention, or purpose, is what drives magical work. You're engaging in magic because you want to achieve something, whether it be creating a certain mental state or effecting change of some kind in your life or in the life of others. Working the magic helps you muster the energy to make this thing, whatever it is, happen. The intention behind a spell or ritual is what determines how the energy raised by your magical activity is directed.

To understand this, let's go back to the example of my friend who asked for a porn star and ended up with a prescription for antibiotics. What he really wanted was love, right? This is something a lot of us want. So my friend found a spell that promised to bring love to him and he performed it. As he performed whatever the steps of the spell were, he pictured what he wanted and he focused on bringing that into his life.

This is what magic is: focusing on what you're trying to

achieve. In the case of "casting" a spell, there's a series of steps you undertake to do the spell. Maybe this involves finding certain ingredients or saying certain words. As you gather these ingredients or say these words, you think about what it is finding the ingredient or saying the words will hopefully achieve for you. The entire time you're working the spell, your thoughts are on accomplishing a particular task.

The ingredients you use will in some way be related to the task at hand, and the words you say are going to be based on what it is you're trying to achieve, but the real power of the spell is that you are concentrating all of your energies on making what you want to happen come true. The lavender you crush up or the rose petals you burn may smell lovely and may represent a particular love goddess, but they don't have any intrinsic power. Their usefulness is as tools to help set a mood, to put your mind in a state where it is focused on the notion of bringing love into your life. Similarly, making a scented bath oil to bathe in for seven nights during the waxing moon isn't the magic. The magic comes from the fact that going through this ritual of making the oil and using it for seven nights keeps your mind focused on finding love.

So why can't you skip all of this and just decide to find love? Why do you need magic? Well, you don't necessarily need magic. But rituals help us create levels of consciousness. They reinforce ideas and help center our thoughts and intentions. This, in turn, can create changes in us that result in different ways of behaving and thinking that eventually result in the changes we're trying to effect.

In the case of doing a love spell, the act of performing the spell puts you in the mind-set to receive love. Perhaps this results in you doing things that put you in a better position to find potential partners or alters the way you approach other people. Certainly, these are all changes you could have made on your own, but by participating in the action of doing the spell you've intensified your intention to find love.

Again, I want to reinforce that magic in and of itself is not what creates the changes you're trying to make. They come from within you. The magic is everything you do to put yourself in a position where what you want can occur.

As a personal example, a number of years ago I came up with the idea for a series of novels for teenagers based on Wiccan themes. I've written many books for this audience, and I was convinced that this series was both needed and sure to be popular. I approached one of my publishers with the idea, convinced she would snap the idea up. She didn't. In fact, she thought my idea was terrible.

I decided that trying a little magic in conjunction with my attempts to sell the series might help, so I devised what I thought was a wonderful ritual to give my efforts a boost. Then I tried another publisher and was once again shot down. Even my agent at the time was less than enthusiastic about the idea.

I knew by then that, as the Rolling Stones said, we don't always get what we want, so I told myself that I was just plain wrong about the series being a good idea. I put it away and went to work on other things. A couple of years went by. Then, completely out of the blue, I received a call from a newly hired editor at the publishing house that had originally rejected the series. Did I, the new editor asked, know anything about Witchcraft? She thought that a series about girls studying Wicca might be good to do and wondered if I might have some thoughts on that.

The end result was a fifteen-book series called Circle of Three, which I wrote under the name Isobel Bird. The books focus on three teenage girls who develop an interest in Witchcraft and seek to find out what it really means (coincidentally, what brings them together is a love spell gone disastrously wrong). Writing the series was one of the best experiences of my life, both personally and professionally, and resulted in thousands of letters from people who discovered Wicca by reading the books.

Now, you could certainly say that magic had nothing to do with the series being published. I disagree. I think that it helped me focus my intention for the series, and then to be patient until the time was right for the books to be published. I am a firm believer in the idea that if you clarify your intentions, and really focus on understanding what it is you want out of a given situation, you will create an atmosphere around you that allows the right things to happen.

When I was involved in the Christian tradition, I often heard people say that if your prayers went unanswered or if the opposite of what you asked for occurred, then God had other plans for you and you should accept it. I think a better response is one suggested by a friend of mine who happens to be an Episcopal priest: maybe you asked for the wrong thing.

Using prayer—or magic—as a kind of wish list for things you want isn't an effective use either. Instead, you should use magic to help you achieve things that really matter. Doing a spell to make you famous, for example, would be a pretty stupid thing to do. The universe isn't some kind of cosmic ATM that dispenses goodies just because you want them. A more mature, responsible use of magic in this instance would be to perform rituals that help you focus on using your talents to the best of your abilities and creating opportunities for you to have your talents noticed.

We've all read the fairy tales about the foolish person who is granted three wishes and chooses badly, only to wind up more unhappy than she or he was at the beginning. That's an example of a bad use of magic. Similarly, my friend who asked for sex with a porn star got it, but at a cost. He misused his intentions, and although he got what he thought he wanted, he paid for it.

This is not to say you can't make requests of the universe or that you have to operate under a system of struggle and reward. The world is filled with opportunities, and it's my belief that whatever might exist in the universe wants us to experience life fully. But Wicca is based on responsibility for our actions. Using our gifts, or the gifts of the universe, for selfish gain is not responsible. And as the Law of Three states, if you send intention out wastefully, or in a misdirected way, it's eventually going to come back to bite you in the ass.

Many people try to cover up their lack of intention with window dressing in the form of theatrics. Your spell didn't work, they might say, because you used a blue candle instead of a white one. You didn't get what you wanted because you failed to do your spell using rosemary grown in your own backyard and watered with your tears. Oh, and by the way, how *dare* you attempt to do magical work wearing that ratty old T-shirt!

I want to whack these fools upside the head with their own Book of Shadows (a Witch's personal journal of spells and magical thoughts). They're missing the whole point. They want someone else, the universe, or whatever deity they involve in their work to do everything for them. They aren't willing to put effort and hard work into their magic or into their lives.

And it *is* effort and hard work. But it's also beautiful, soothing, and energizing depending on what it is you're doing. We use the word *energy* a lot in metaphysical discussions, and it's true that sometimes the word is thrown around when there's no substantive way of describing something. "He has such wonderful energy," someone says, or "Your negative energy is making it really hard for me to feel good about myself."

It may sound nutty sometimes, but the fact is, energy exists in everything and it does affect us. Intention is energy. It's emotional energy we raise to help us achieve something, emotional energy that then becomes physical energy to create change or accomplish a task. It's amazing what we can achieve when we set our minds to it. With strong enough intention, things that can easily seem overwhelming or even impossible suddenly seem doable. We find that we have undiscovered stores of strength to make things happen.

Apart from my writing, I teach scuba diving. I love the ocean, and I love introducing people to the world that exists beneath the waves. Often, I have students who are, for various reasons, absolutely terrified of getting in the water. I could spend a lot of time explaining how safe diving is (more people are killed each year by coconuts falling on their heads than by participating in diving) and using facts to calm their fears. I could simply tell them to get over it, to suck it up and do the skills they need to do to become certified divers. And they might do it. But I guarantee you they wouldn't enjoy it, and probably they would never go back in the water again.

Instead, what I do is have them sit and meditate. I tell them to close their eyes and imagine themselves under the water. I describe for them the things they might see when we go to the ocean. Then I walk them through the various skills they need to do, having them picture each and every one and imagining themselves doing the skills easily and without any fear.

Invariably, these students have a great time. They come up from their dives excited about their newfound skills and excited about the things they've seen underwater. Is this magic? Of a kind. By tapping into parts of themselves they hadn't explored before, the students create an atmosphere in which they can succeed. By focusing their energy and intention, they see themselves enjoying the dives and doing the necessary skills easily, and then they find themselves doing exactly that.

With students who are also Pagan or Wiccan, I might go even further. For them I might create a more elaborate ritual involving gods and goddesses related to the sea. I might remind them that the ocean is a perfect example of how all of creation is connected and how we know less about what's in the ocean than we do about what's on the moon. I could relate their scuba diving to entering a mysterious world where they can come face to face with the divine.

It's the same thing, only in the second example I'm incorporating the decorations of Witchcraft and creating an experience that will resonate with someone who considers him- or herself a Witch. As we've discussed previously, what we call magic in Wicca is similar to what other religions may call by other names, such as prayer or asking God for help. When it's practiced by Witches, however, it takes on magical overtones because that's how we view it within our belief system.

What, then, are the parameters of magic? What can and can't you use it for? That's up to you. It's all about how you personally see the Wiccan Rede and the Law of Three as they apply to you. The important thing when considering the use of magic is whether or not you're willing to live with the possible consequences.

There are people who believe that it's perfectly okay to ask for anything they might possibly want, such as sex, money, or fame. There are people who claim that using magic has helped them to achieve these things, and I have no reason to disbelieve them. As I've said, I think you can pretty much achieve whatever you want if you set your mind to it. But I will say that, in my personal experience, these people are not happy, productive, genuinely thoughtful individuals who are making a positive difference in the world in which they live. Yes, you can use magic for revenge or to get things you don't honestly deserve. A true Witch, however, would not use magic for destructive ends. To again quote one of Clarke's characters, this time the magician Mr. Strange answering a fictionalized Lord Wellington's query about whether a magician could kill an enemy with magic, "I suppose a magician might, but a gentleman never could."

The times I've seen magic have the greatest effect are when it has been used to accomplish something that truly benefits an individual, a group, or the larger world. For example, a Witch friend of mine, diagnosed with inoperable cancer, asked some of us to do magic on her behalf. She didn't ask to be cured. She didn't ask for everything to be "all right." She simply asked us to do magic for her.

One Witch suggested a ritual we could do either as individuals or as a group. It involved using a ball of soap to represent our friend's cancer. The magic was to be washing that ball of soap in water scented with whatever herbs or oils we found pleasing and imaging our friend's cancer—and the accompanying physical pain and emotional distress—diminishing as the soap ball became smaller and smaller.

This was a beautiful suggestion and one we all happily undertook. Did our friend's cancer go away? No. But in the months before her death, she experienced deep feelings of love and acceptance because she knew so many people were working magic on her behalf. Her physical pain did abate to some degree, but the important changes occurred within her. And those of us who joined her in this extended magical web also felt ourselves changed, both in our relationships to her and in our relationships to our own bodies and to our feelings about sickness and death.

Skeptics will read these thoughts on magic and roll their

eyes, believing that what I'm calling magic could just as well have been achieved by visits to a physician or psychiatrist, or simply by putting one's priorities in order. And perhaps that's true. But we all achieve things in our lives in different ways, and for some of us the practice of magic is the most powerful way to become the people we want to be.

Unfortunately, there are people in the Witch community—just as there are people in every spiritual community—who misrepresent what magic is and who don't understand the principles behind it. Just as we would (I hope) agree that praying to God for the destruction of your enemies isn't exactly a positive thing to do, I would hope we would agree that using magic to manipulate other people is not something that fits within the guidelines of the Rede. "Making" someone fall in love with you, for example, is vastly different from performing a spell to invite love into your life. Could you force someone to fall in love with you? There are people who claim they've done it, and if you can focus your energy enough I don't see why it couldn't be done. But at what cost? What would the love of someone who doesn't truly love you of his own free will really bring you?

It should be pointed out, too, that being Wiccan doesn't automatically mean you practice magic, just as practicing magic doesn't necessarily mean you're Wiccan. Magic is something that people do because they feel it grows naturally out of their personal spiritual path. Personally, I think magic should be used judiciously and only after careful thought. As part of the overall Path of the Green Man, I see magic as being a very small part of a larger spiritual expression.

Remember, too, that magic doesn't have to be about getting something. It can also be—and most often is—about achieving a state of consciousness. Sometimes, you may use magical work to calm yourself down or, conversely, fire yourself up. Often, before I begin a new writing project, I create a ritual that has something do with whatever it is I'm working on. Doing this helps me focus on what it is I want to achieve with the project at hand, and it also puts me in the mood to write, both of which contribute greatly to getting me to actually put words down on paper. Similarly, if I'm having a day when I feel stressed and out of control, I may take some time to do a simple centering and calming ritual, which is almost guaranteed to put things into perspective and put me in a better state of mind.

As you progress on your spiritual journey, you may use magic to create different kinds of moods: relaxed, joyful, energized, or meditative are all states you can induce through magical work. The whirling dervishes—who are Sufi Muslims—are renowned for their ability to enter trance-like states through their beautiful, spinning dances. People adept at meditation can enter states where both physical and emotional energy levels are greatly changed. These are all forms of what we are calling magic.

By now you've undoubtedly noticed that I haven't given any real specifics about *how* magic is done. That will come in the next few chapters. For now what's important is that you have a basic understanding of how magic is viewed, at least in the Green Man tradition. I do, however, want to end this chapter with what I consider one of the most basic magical rituals. I encourage you to try it and then, when you feel ready, move on to other rituals discussed later in the book.

Exercise: A Spell to Open the Door

When most people think about magic, they think about being able to do wondrous things simply by saying some words or performing certain rituals. But in reality magic is about focusing your intentions and using the energy within yourself and within nature to help you achieve a goal. To perform magic properly and successfully, you have to be able to work with this energy. That takes time and practice, just as it takes time and practice to learn how to ride a bike, play a piece on the piano, or paint a picture. Being able to work magic requires the same discipline and practice as any other skill or art, and the best way to begin to learn how to work with energy is to start with the following basic exercise.

Step 1: Find a quiet place where you won't be disturbed by anyone. This could be your bedroom or another room in your home or a place outdoors, such as under a favorite tree or beside a pond. The important thing is that it be someplace where no one will bother you and where you will feel totally comfortable sitting for some time with your eyes closed. Be sure to wear comfortable clothing that doesn't pinch or restrict your breathing. If possible, remove your shoes.

Step 2: Sit quietly with your legs folded and your hands in your lap. Close your eyes. Be very still and breathe slowly, feeling the air enter your body when you inhale and leave it again when you exhale. Feel your heart beating and allow yourself to relax. Let your weight rest on the earth as if you're being held in a giant hand.

Step 3: When you feel relaxed, imagine yourself in an outdoor place that makes you feel happy and secure. This can be the actual place where you're sitting or some other place, real or imagined. What's important is that it be a place that *you* love and feel welcome in. Many people like to imagine themselves in a circle of trees or stones, while others find mountaintops, meadows, or the seashore to be good choices. Imagine a place that calls to you. If you have trouble thinking of one, just sit quietly for a few more minutes. Something will come to you. And remember, there are no right or wrong places. Whatever comes to mind is where you need to be.

Step 4: When you've imagined your setting, sit for a while and let yourself "see" that place. Really look at the details. What kind of trees are in your circle? How does the air smell? What season is it in your magical place? Get to know this place, because chances are you'll be returning to it again and again in your magical work.

Step 5: When you feel settled in your magical space, return to focusing on your breathing. When you feel completely relaxed, place your palms on the floor (if you're inside) or ground (if you're outside) either in front of you or to your sides. Now imagine that small roots are growing down into the ground from your hands, as well as from your legs and bottom where they touch the floor or ground. These roots are connecting you to the earth, digging deep into the rich brown soil. Imagine them growing longer and longer, reaching down into the ground until they come to pools of bright white light. When they reach the light, imagine it touching the roots and traveling back up them until it reaches your body. Then imagine the light entering your body, filling you up with warmth and energy. In your mind, see the light fill you like a glass, coursing through your veins and becoming part of you. You are drawing light, energy, and strength up from the earth.

Step 6: When you feel yourself completely filled with the white light, bring your hands up and hold them together in your lap. Sit quietly and imagine yourself glowing with the energy you've raised from the earth. It is part of you, and it connects you to the world around you. Let it flow through your body and pay attention to how it makes you feel. You might actually be able to feel it flowing through your fingertips from one hand to the other, but if you don't, that's okay. The important thing is that you visualize the light filling you and being part of you. Think about how you are connected to the earth and how you drew the energy up from the ground. Think about this same energy flowing through everything and how it may have been flowing through trees, rocks, or animals before it came to you. If you're feeling sad, angry, or frustrated about something, let the white light burn away these feelings and replace them with feelings of happiness and contentedness.

Step 7: When you feel ready, prepare to release the energy back into the world. You can do this in several ways. You can place your palms on the floor or ground again and imagine the white light flowing out of you and back into the ground like water. You can also hold your hands up and imagine the energy flowing out of your fingers and into the air, where it is swept away by the winds. Or you can cup your hands together and imagine the light filling them, forming a shining ball that you then toss into the air so that it explodes like fireworks. Again, there's no wrong way to release the energy. The important thing is that you return it to nature, where it can be reabsorbed and reused. And when you do return it, know that part of *your* energy has gone with it and is now added to that of everything else in nature. At the same time, you've also kept some of the collective energy within you.

This exercise is very simple, and you might think it hasn't accomplished anything. But it has done two important things.

First, it's helped you imagine a magical place where you will probably find yourself returning again and again as you practice more ritual and magic. Many people find that the place they imagine themselves in during this exercise becomes very important to them. Often, it's a place they return to on a daily basis when they meditate or when they need to feel themselves in a safe place where they can just sit and be quiet or do magic. You may want to write down what the place looked like and what you saw there. The more you visit it, the more details you'll discover, and it's interesting to see how your personal magical place changes the more you go there.

The second thing this exercise has done is help you learn how to draw energy into yourself and release it again, and this will form the basis of all the magical work you ever do. After this exercise you might feel elated or very relaxed. You might also feel hungry, in which case you should eat something like a cookie or drink a glass of juice to help "ground" you. You've experienced what coming into contact with energy—both from outside and within yourself—can do, and this can have a powerful and lasting effect. Remember that you've tapped into the energy that unites all things and know that you can do this whenever you need or want to. The more you do this exercise, the easier it will be. Eventually, you will find that filling yourself with energy becomes a natural reflex, like catching a ball or knowing where to put your fingers when you play an instrument.

This is the most basic of all magical exercises, and it's one that will help you develop your powers of concentration and focus if you do it regularly. From there you can move on to other exercises. But this is the first one you need to master. It is one of the easiest and most useful ways to open the door to the world of magic. Now that you've done it, step inside and see what awaits you.

A NIGHT IN MAEVE'S WOOD

A Story for Litha

ABOUT LITHA

Interestingly, I've found nothing about the origin of the word *litha* except the suggestion that at some point it was used to refer to the entire season of summer and eventually came to be applied specifically to the date of the summer solstice. Whatever the origin of its name, Litha is the longest day of the year, the transition from the waxing year to the waning year. It is also the day on which the Oak King, the god of the waxing year, dies and is replaced by the Holly King, the god of the waning year.

The Oak King and the Holly King are traditionally seen as twin brothers. The story goes that at Litha the Oak King is either slain by his brother or ritually sacrificed by his people to ensure a good harvest. The reverse occurs at Yule, when the Oak King regains the throne for his half of the year. This seems a little grim, but there you are.

Litha, or Midsummer, is traditionally associated with the faerie realm. On this most magical of nights, the faerie queen, Maeve, holds court deep in the woods and she and her followers dance and sing to celebrate the height of summer. Much folklore surrounds Midsummer, and it has long been believed to be a night on which the most powerful spells may be cast.

In this story, I combine these traditions to create something I think is most relevant to queer men: acknowledging our gifts and then accepting the responsibility of using them well. In meeting Maeve, the Green Man finds himself taking part in the ancient tradition of marking the transition between the two halves of the Wheel of the Year. In doing so, he also acknowledges the work he has done in the first half and looks ahead to the second half. And by making the mask of what he hopes to become, he gives form to his desires, which is the most potent magic of all. What would your mask look like?

AS TWILIGHT FELL on the longest day of the year, the Green Man found himself wandering far from home. He had risen early that morning with a desire to walk to a part of the valley he had yet to visit, and by afternoon he had lost himself among the hills and vales. Yet even though darkness would soon cover the land, he was not afraid. He knew that the way home would appear when he needed it, and he had spent more than one night asleep under the stars. He had food in his pack and water in the stream he walked beside, and the whole of the world was his waiting bed.

It happened that as the sun and moon passed one another in the sky, the Green Man came to a wood. Deciding to take his rest beneath one of the trees casting shade over the mossy ground, he made his way among them until he came to a clearing. The circle was filled with the scent of bluebells, and the Green Man was made drowsy by their smell. While he knew it was foolish for any mortal to spend even half an hour within a faerie circle, he found himself unable to keep his eyes open. He lay among the flowers and soon was dreaming of wild things.

He awoke with a start to the tinkling of bells. When he opened his heavy lids, he saw that it was dark. Moonlight flooded the circle and gilded the leaves with silver, and for a moment he saw only the shadows flitting against the pale backdrop like figures in a pantomime.

Then a light sparked before his eyes, followed by another, and still others. Fireflies floated in the air around him, moving lazily in the warm night like tiny boats on the sea. They danced away from him and stopped, as if waiting for him to follow. Somewhere beyond the edge of the clearing he heard laughter.

The Green Man stood, rubbing the sleep from his eyes. The fireflies rose and encircled him, casting a pale ring of light. They flew forward, gently urging him on, and he found himself walking out of the clearing and onto a narrow path he couldn't remember seeing during the day.

The path led deep into the woods, and the Green Man was glad for the light of the fireflies as he found himself walking between towering trees whose branches hid the moon from view. As he walked, he heard the merry sound of the bells from time to time, and every now and again a laugh would reach his ears.

Suddenly, the path took a turn and opened into another clearing. Here, the moonlight was bright, and the Green Man had to shield his eyes. As he did, the fireflies around him rose up and exploded in bursts of gold. When the Green Man was able to see again, he found that he was surrounded by a host of faeries. They darted around him, and he knew then where the laughter he had heard came from. Their voices were rich and merry, and they all talked at once so that the sound was like that of moth wings in his ears.

He stood, watching, as the faeries filled the clearing with their beauty. They swooped and twirled in interlocking circles, some with wings like those of dragonflies, some with butterfly wings, and some with no wings at all. He had heard the tales of these creatures and had even believed them. But to see them before him was to be enchanted beyond words or movement.

"They were right in saying that you were fair," said a voice from within the swirling lights.

The golden, whirling cloud of faeries parted like curtains being drawn aside, and the Green Man saw standing before him a woman of unearthly beauty. Her skin was the color of lilies, and her eyes the green of deep water. Her hair was black like a winter night and fell about her shoulders in curls that trailed to the ground. On her head was a crown of roses and lavender, and her dress was of the palest silver, as though woven from cobwebs and moonlight.

"It is not every mortal who is invited to my midsummer gathering," said the woman. "How came you to lie in the circle where my servants found you?"

"I am sorry," said the Green Man, afraid of having offended the lady. "I was tired, and wanted only to rest."

She smiled cooly. "Those who sleep on my doorstep often find more than rest," she said. "Answer me this: Would you be my king?"

The Green Man lowered his head. "I am no king," he said. "I am but an ordinary man."

Laughter filled the clearing as the faeries flew like gusts of summer wind. The Green Man looked up and saw that the lady was laughing with them.

"No one is ordinary who is brought to the court of Maeve," she said. "Come and join us."

The faeries once more darted around the clearing, filling it with blinding light. When the light died, the Green Man saw that the place was decorated as if for a grand feast. A table made from a fallen tree was spread with leaves and mounded high with good things to eat. The branches were hung with lights, and music came from somewhere in the treetops as unseen players piped and fiddled.

The Green Man saw, too, that they were no longer alone in the clearing. Guests filled the spaces between the trees and circled the edge of the place. Each wore a mask, and it was impossible for the Green Man to tell if behind the faces they were human or something more. A great owl-headed woman stood beside a man with the ears of a hare, while elsewhere a trio of goat-legged boys played on silver flutes. As the Green Man looked at them, he saw that each was more fantastic than the next, and all gazed back at him where he stood beside the faerie queen.

Maeve took the Green Man by the hand and led him to the table crowded with revelers. He seated himself beside a man with the laughing face of a bear, and the attending faeries set before him a cup filled with sweet wine. He drank it as he reclined in the soft moss and waited to see what would happen next.

Maeve returned to the center of the circle and clapped her hands together once. "Enter the Oak King," she commanded.

There was a rustling in the trees and then a man stepped into the clearing. He was dressed in clothes of deepest gold, and on his head was a crown of oak leaves, heavy with acorns. His face was covered by a mask showing the brilliant face of a shining sun, so that the Green Man could not see his features. He carried in his hand a staff of gnarled wood, and he walked slowly toward the faerie queen as though coming to the end of a long journey.

"Merry meet," she said when he reached her, holding out her hands to him. "It is long since you began your reign. Now it is time for rest."

She clapped her hands in the air once more, and the musicians began to play a slow but steady rhythm. The Green Man watched as Maeve took the hand of the Oak King and the two danced. Their movements were gentle, like the slow ripple of the wind through the ripening fields. Hand in hand, they traveled the edge of the circle, moving in the direction of the sun through the sky.

After they had made one tour of the clearing, the music began to increase in time and the guests joined their queen. They danced around the Oak King, still masked, who was spun from hand to waiting hand as he was guided in his steps. Many times he was passed around the circle by the faerie queen's guests, until finally he was brought, breathless, back to the center to the waiting queen. She took him in her arms and placed a kiss on his mouth, after which he collapsed to the ground.

"The Oak King is dead," cried the queen, and the crowd was silent.

Again, there was a rustling in the trees and in came six men dressed in gold. They carried on their shoulders a litter made of birch branches and decorated with summer flowers that filled the air with their scent. They came to the place where the fallen king lay and lowered the litter to the ground. Then they gathered the king into their arms and laid him on the litter.

Maeve bent over the Oak King's face and removed the golden mask. As she did, the Green Man gasped, for he saw his own familiar features, stilled in death. Maeve motioned to him and smiled.

"Come," she said. "It is time for you to take his place."

The Green Man rose to his feet and stepped forward, not believing what he saw before him. He approached the Oak King and stood beside his body.

"How can this be?" he asked.

Maeve looked into his eyes. "Remember," she said, "you are in *my* kingdom now. This is the night when the wild magic runs strong, the time when the waxing year and the waning year meet. You will see much here that you would not see in your world. But fear nothing."

"What am I to do?" the Green Man said.

"You are to take your place as Holly King," Maeve told him. "The king of the waning year. Until now you have learned much about who you are. You have followed the year as it grew to fullness. Now it is time to use that knowledge, to come into the fullness of your self and celebrate all that you have learned.

But first you must make your own mask like that of the Oak King."

She gestured to the table at which the Green Man had been sitting, and he saw that the food and drink had been replaced by piles of flowers, leaves, stones, and feathers. He walked over to it as Maeve spoke.

"Create the face you wish to show to the world," she said. "Make manifest your own vision of who you are, for this is the night of giving birth to our true selves. Show us who you are beneath your skin."

The Green Man knelt and began to make his mask. He formed a covering of holly leaves, dark and shining. To this he affixed different items as he was drawn to them, building one on the other until he had before him the face he saw when he dreamed. His hands did the work of his heart, and soon he was finished. Then he picked up his mask and carried it to where Maeve stood waiting.

"It is beautiful," she said as he held it up for all to see. She took the ends of the ribbons attached to the mask and secured them around the Green Man's head.

"Now," she said, "we will make the magic real."

At the queen's signal, the faeries fluttered around the Green Man. They stripped him of his traveling clothes and placed on him robes of green and red. On his head they placed a crown of holly and evergreens.

"Dance with me, Holly King," said Maeve when they were finished, and the music began.

The Green Man took her hand and followed as she led him around the circle. The sound of the faerie drums and bells filled his ears, and he stepped lightly with his queen. The faerie court sang and laughed, watching their new king dancing in the moonlight, and the Green Man laughed with them. In their midst, he felt filled with the possibilities of magic. He looked at the Oak King where he lay on his deathbed in the center of the ring, and he knew that it had taken much to become that part of himself. Now it was time to take on the mantle of the Holly King and step into the darkening year.

The music played and the Green Man danced on, faster and faster. He saw those around him through new eyes and felt the magic coursing in his veins. His head swam with the sound of voices and music, and he closed his eyes and lost himself in the whirling magic of midsummer night until he no longer knew if he were sleeping or awake.

When finally the music ceased, the Green Man opened his eyes and found himself alone in the woods. The night was gone, and the first faint stirrings of sunlight crept across the dewy grass where he stood. Gone was Maeve and her curious faerie court. Gone were the red and green robes. And gone, too, was the Oak King and his attendants. Only the Green Man remained, still wearing the mask of his creation and feeling the magic spinning within him.

The shortest night of the year had ended, and the drawing in of the days had begun. The faerie queen and her court had seen in another king and carried an old one away with them for renewal. Now was the time of the Holly King. As the Green Man walked into the morning, he carried his mask in his hands and the memories of his night in Maeve's woods in his heart.

Chapter 6

Exploring the Wheel
of the Year

As you have gathered by now, the life of a Pagan person (whether Witch or not) is centered around nature. Pagan spirituality has its origins in humankind's attempts to understand and relate to the natural world. Deities were created to explain natural occurrences and celebrations were instituted to commemorate these deities and the cycles of nature with which they were associated, all of which were inextricably tied to the lives of the people who lived in such close connection with the land.

This ever-repeating cycle of nature—planting and harvesting, light and dark, birth and death—is symbolized by what we call the Wheel of the Year. If you have been reading "The Journey of the Green Man" in this book, you have already gotten some sense of what the Wheel of the Year is. Each season represents part of the natural cycle, and each season has its own important days that Pagan people recognize.

There are eight celebration days—called sabbats—that comprise the Wheel of the Year. Four of these dates are sometimes called the Greater Sabbats, and four are sometimes called the

Lesser Sabbats, although really all eight sabbats are equal in importance, as they represent equally important principles of Pagan spirituality. The four Lesser Sabbats are the two equinoxes and the two solstices of the year, occurring on or about March 21 (the vernal equinox, also called Ostara), June 21 (the summer solstice, also called Litha), September 21 (the autumn equinox, also called Mabon), and December 21 (the winter solstice, also called Yule). The four Greater Sabbats are the holidays (or holy days, if you will) of Imbolc (February 1), Beltane (May 1), Lammas (August 1), and Samhain (October 31). We will discuss each sabbat individually and look at the role it plays in Pagan spirituality.

Observing the dates of the Wheel of the Year is an excellent way to strengthen your connection to the cycles of nature, which in turn will help you develop a deeper understanding of your place in the world. Most of us don't live as closely tied to nature as our ancestors did, although we maintain some of these connections in different forms. Gardeners, for example, are very much aware of the cycles of planting, growth, and death. Those of us who engage in outdoor activities are conscious of the seasonal changes in weather, and even those of us who pay little attention to nature apart from checking whether or not we need to carry an umbrella, put snow tires on the car, or apply sunscreen are aware that there is a seasonal cycle.

Often, though, these are the only thoughts we give to what these cycles represent. But by paying greater attention to the Wheel of the Year and how it mirrors cycles (both emotional and physical) in our own lives, we return to that time when people and nature were not quite so apart from one another. Sometimes, I think a number of the sabbats are rather similar. How many times, I think to myself, do we have to be reminded to create, to be thankful, or to take time to just sit and take it all in? But when I stop to really experience them, I see that each sabbat comes at a time when I need that renewing reminder. With that in mind, let's take a look at the sabbats one by one and see how celebrating them is a part of the Path of the Green Man.

Yule (on or about December 21)

In Pagan chronology, the sabbat of Samhain (what we know as Halloween and will be discussed later in this chapter) is New Year's Eve. Seen that way, the sabbat of Yule is the first station of the Wheel of the Year. This is the winter solstice, the date on which the hours of darkness are the longest.

For people living without the benefit of electric light or central heating, the coming of winter was a very serious thing. It signified a period during which life stopped. Animals went into hibernation. Nothing grew. Darkness seemed almost constant. For people who saw the world very much as a living entity, it seemed that the earth had gone to sleep, perhaps even died.

On a theological-mythological level, Yule can be viewed as something of a low point, a time when the world seems plunged in darkness. Yet, within the cold and dark there is hope. The sun is waiting to be born, existing as a faint memory. It is our job to awaken the sun, to call it back through the darkness, to give it strength so that it can grow stronger and warmer and reawaken the life that lies sleeping in the earth.

For many of us, this is indeed a time of cold and darkness. A number of people experience depression and sadness in the winter, or perhaps less intense feelings of restlessness and dissatisfaction. It is often a time of withdrawing from life and waiting for summer. Rather than wishing that winter would pass more quickly, it is more useful to see it as a time of rest and renewal. Celebrating Yule helps us do this.

I once attended a beautiful Yule service at the Cathedral of

St. John the Divine in New York City. My friend Katherine and I arrived there at some early hour, I think three or four in the morning. For several hours performers sang, danced, and played instruments in celebration of the sun. When the real sun finally broke through the winter sky, a lone musician greeted it with a merry tune. It was a really lovely way to celebrate the end of the longest night.

Christmas, obviously, is a variation on Yule, with the birth of the sun being replaced by the birth of the Son of God. Although this appropriation of the Pagan holiday is more than slightly manipulative, the shared principle is one of hope: a radiant power has come to us to drive the cold and dark away for a time.

Yule can be celebrated in many ways. Some people like to gather friends around and welcome the light back with eating, drinking, and laughing. Some prefer a more somber celebration of meditation and reflection on what it means to awaken the light within ourselves during times of darkness. Still others like to physically connect with the winter, going outside to dance in the snow or otherwise be in direct connection with nature. I myself have always thought it would be great fun to spend Yule in Alaska, taking a dogsled to a mountain retreat and watching the gorgeous aurora borealis fill the sky.

However you celebrate Yule, the point is to think about light returning to your life and to consider how you can use the winter—a time of darkness and reflection—to prepare for the months ahead. What projects do you want to work on? How would you like to change your life? What can you do to awaken the light within you? These are questions you can ask yourself at this time of year.

For the first Green Men Yule celebration, I wrote the following song-poem that represented, to me, what we were trying to do with that first ritual together.

Green Men Yule Song

The god is in the winter wood,
our circle gathers near.
The fire burns, the Horned One turns
the Wheel of the Year.
Welcome winter, ages old,
welcome nights of dark and cold,
welcome spirits bringing snow,
welcome winds that rush and blow.

The god is in the winter wood,
we listen for his song.
He calls the sun back with his voice
to make the days grow long.
Welcome sun, the child of light,
welcome morning, shining bright,
welcome hope and joy restored,
welcome life, reborn once more.

Imbolc (February 1)

Meaning roughly "in the belly," Imbolc is said to be a reference to pregnant ewes, mother sheep whose bodies carried lambs and who were preparing to produce milk to feed their young ones. It is a time when the world is preparing itself for life after the barren cold of winter. The festival itself was dedicated to the Celtic goddess Brigid, a deity whose popularity among the people was unequaled (Christianity would later turn Brigid into Mary, a form in which she would continue to be deeply venerated).

A fire goddess associated with beauty, poetry, and the warmth of a home filled with love and light, Brigid was the perfect symbol for this sabbat. Weary of the long winter, people would be looking ahead to the spring, their thoughts filled with plans for the future. This was a time for quickening those plans, for strengthening intention and raising energy to fuel them before giving birth to them (as the ewes did to their lambs). The fire tended by Brigid, and the cauldron in which she worked her magic, became the inspiration for the bonfires that traditionally were lit throughout the land to celebrate this sabbat.

Because Imbolc is associated with the milk produced by ewes for their lambs, some people like to create rituals and celebrations centered around milk and things made with milk. The ritual created by Green Men members for this sabbat included passing around pieces of cheese, which sounds a bit silly, but actually was very powerful (and tasty). Also, because Imbolc is a time of inspiration, I created an exercise in which various inspirational words we called the Words of Power were written on pieces of paper and placed in a bowl. Each man picked a word from the bowl, with the idea being that the chosen word represented something he was to work on in the time between Imbolc and the next sabbat. The words we used were:

accept	challenge	desire
allow	chance	discover
ask	change	do
awaken	choice	dream
aware	commit	embark
begin	compassion	embrace
believe	conceive	emerge
belong	create	family
build	dance	feed
care	dare	forgive
celebrate	defy	friends

fulfill	observe	remember
give	open	renew
growth	own	risk
heal	plan	search
inspire	plant	share
invite	play	shine
join	praise	song
journey	promise	spirit
joy	question	teach
kindness	quiet	touch
laugh	rebirth	trust
light	receive	unfold
listen	reclaim	weave
live	recover	welcome
love	reflect	withdraw
magic	rejoice	wonder
music	release	write
nurture		

The word I selected when it was my turn was *risk*. Interestingly, at the time I was thinking seriously about putting some of my thoughts on Green Man spirituality in written form, but thought the project might be too difficult. After receiving this word in the ritual, I began to do so, and now six years later the results of that inspiration are this book.

Ostara (on or around March 21)

A celebration in honor of the Saxon goddess Eostre, the spring equinox is a time of birth and life. The sun, conceived at Yule and coming to term at Imbolc, is born at Ostara. In celebration, nature awakens, crops and flowers emerge from the earth, and animals begin the cycle of birth and death by having their young.

When it came time to create the first Green Men Ostara ritual, we decided to make it all-out fun. We decorated the room with chocolate bunnies, candles, and drifts of brightly colored fabric. Participants dressed in bright, fun clothes, and the whole atmosphere was, as I recall, very childlike and playful. The ritual itself began with drumming and singing, which added to the festive mood.

The majority of the ritual was devoted to two craft-oriented activities. The first was something I call Oracle Eggs. I wanted to incorporate the egg symbol into our ritual, as it both symbolizes the sun and is representative of birth and creativity. For the Oracle Eggs, I carefully emptied plain old chicken eggs, placed a slip of paper that had one of the Words of Power used in our Imbolc ritual written on it inside the egg, and then painted each egg with images I felt represented the sabbat.

We passed around a bowl of eggs and each Green Man chose an egg he was attracted to. The egg, with the Word of Power still inside, was placed on his personal altar at home. Even without knowing what the word was, each man was encouraged to imagine whatever was inside the egg growing and coming to fruition in the time between Ostara and the next sabbat, Beltane. At Beltane, if they chose, they could break their egg to see what word was inside it and to send the energy they'd created by meditating on the egg and the word inside it into the universe. Others chose to leave their egg intact and continue to meditate on it, believing that doing so would manifest whatever word was contained inside in their lives (and since all the words were positive ones, it didn't really matter if they ever knew exactly which word they'd chosen).

Ostara Oracle Eggs

MATERIALS:

Eggs
Seam ripper or other sharp object for making holes in eggs
Gesso (artist's plaster available at most craft stores)
Newspaper or tissue paper
Small quantity of paste made of equal parts white glue and
    water
Paintbrushes
Acrylic paints

Step 1: Take as many uncooked eggs as you need and blow them out. To do this, make a hole in each end of the egg. You can use a pin, but I find a seam ripper works better because the handle is easier to hold and control. Make the first hole in the narrow end of the egg, then make a slightly larger one in the other end. I do this by making two or three holes near one another and using the seam ripper to gently chip away the connecting material. It doesn't have to be huge, but large enough to get a small rolled up piece of paper through.

Step 2: Blow into the narrow end of the egg until the white and yolk come out the other end. Once the egg is empty, run water through it and blow it out again, then let it dry.

Step 3: Write your Words of Power (or whatever you want to write) on small slips (about 2 inches by 1/4 inch) of paper. Fold the paper into a narrow strip, or roll it around a toothpick to make a tube of sorts. Then push it through the large hole in the bottom of the egg. This takes some practice, but believe me, it can be done.

Step 4: To seal the holes, I use gesso, a pastelike plaster that is used for preparing canvases for painting. You can get a small jar at any artist supply or craft store. A little dab covers the small hole in the egg. For the larger hole, take small pieces of newspaper or tissue paper, dip them in a mixture of equal parts white glue and water (as if for making papier-mâché), and lay them over the hole. When they dry, cover the area with gesso.

Step 5: When the gesso is dry, paint the eggs a solid base color with acrylic paint. Fabric and crafts stores usually have a wide selection of such paints, and they're cheap. Buy lots! Also get several paintbrushes in various sizes.

Step 6: Once your base coat is dry, go wild. I like to use large, primitive designs in black paint and filled in with dots of bright color to form patterns. Do whatever you want. Paint goddesses, gods, shaman figures, and spirals. Paint snakes, spiders, dogs, and totem animals. Paint suns, moons, stars, and comets. Do whatever inspires you. And don't worry if it doesn't come out the way you want it to. You can always paint it over again.

Once your Oracle Eggs are dry, you can use them in your Ostara rituals in any way you like. Hide them and have an Oracle Egg hunt. Dress up like the Ostara Bunny and hand them out. Or just put them on your altar and use them as meditative tools.

Make Your Own God or Goddess

The second project we undertook during that first Ostara ritual was to make god or goddess statues from salt dough. One of the things I really love is statues. But they are frequently expensive, and you can't always find exactly what you want. When I decided that I wanted to make a representation of Gaia, the earth goddess and symbol of the world, I thought about the fun I had as a kid making salt dough figures. I decided the same thing could be used to make wonderful ritual objects. And the more I thought about it, the more perfect it seemed. What better way to honor a deity than by creating an image of it? And what better medium to use than dough formed from salt, flour, water, and your own hands?

The following recipe made enough dough to form a very zaftig Gaia statue about six inches high. You can use the same proportions to make more or less dough.

3 cups flour (plain white flour)
3 cups salt (Kosher works best)
¾ to 1 cup water

Step 1: Mix the flour and salt together in a bowl (you can use an electric mixer if you want, but I like the added magic of using my hands). Add the water gradually, starting with about half a cup. Mix it into the flour and salt until you have a nice firm dough that you can work easily without it sticking to your hands or to the bowl. You might use more or less water, depending on your flour and on the humidity in the room in which you're working. The important thing is to add only a little at a time. If you add too much and your dough becomes too sticky, simply add a little more flour.

Step 2: Once your dough is formed, place it on a hard surface and knead it until it's good and workable. If it dries and cracks while you're working it, add a little more water and knead it in. The dough should be elastic enough to form into shapes. If you want, you may cover the dough with plastic wrap and let it sit for half an hour to let the gluten in the flour break down even more, making it more elastic.

Step 3: Once you have your dough, go to town. It can be formed into almost any shape. I prefer to start with one big lump of dough and mold it into a shape, rather than trying to make individual parts and sticking them together. This works best, of course, when you want to make nice zaftig goddesses with soft curves. But with a little patience, you can make almost anything. Use your fingers, spoons, knives, or whatever you think of to shape the dough. I find that an orange stick (the thin wooden sticks used to push back cuticles) works great for forming mouths and eyes and other details.

You can't really go wrong with this one. Have fun. Use your imagination and let whatever deity you're creating work through you. You'll probably find that the dough starts taking shape quickly. Don't fuss with it too much or it will start to crack. But if you need to, you can wet it a little and smooth out any rough edges.

Step 4: Once your statue is formed, it needs to dry. You can let it air dry, but this takes forever, and with a thick statue it will probably never really dry. For my statue, I heated the oven to about 200 degrees, set the statue on a piece of tinfoil, and put her in there for about five hours. She dried well on the outside (she cracked a little, which could probably be prevented by using a lower temperature), but was still doughy inside. I didn't intend to keep her forever (I put her outside in the garden to return her to her home), I just wanted her to be dry enough to sit on my altar.

If you want to keep your statue, you will need to heat it for longer. The recommended time is about an hour for every half inch of thickness. So a six-inch statue like mine would take almost twelve hours in the oven to totally dry. Since the heat is so low, this isn't a big deal. You can always put it in overnight and have a nice crispy goddess awaiting you in the morning.

Step 5: Once your statue is dry, you can paint it, decorate it, or do whatever you want to it. If you want to keep it, you'll have to seal it with varnish.

Beltane (May 1)

With the possible exception of Samhain, Beltane is the most misunderstood of the sabbats. Beltane celebrates the beginning of summer and traditionally was a time when inhibitions were cast aside and participants celebrated the beauty of sex, fertility, and procreation. In some instances this involved couples joining together in the fields, the idea being that making love there would inspire the earth to bring forth a bounteous crop.

You can see how this might upset the more prudish among the population, particularly as it seems Beltane revelers were not always particular about who their partners were. For those who weren't entirely comfortable casting off their clothes and coupling atop the earth, there were more chaste (but still extremely provocative) rituals, most notably the tradition of the maypole.

The maypole was undeniably a phallic symbol, a tall, straight pole erected in a meadow or clearing, topped with a garland of flowers and decorated with ribbons. Around the maypole dancers circled while holding the ends of the ribbons, weaving over and under each other's arms until the pole was wrapped tightly with the ribbons and the dancers were hot and exhausted from the exertion. The sexual symbolism is impossible to ignore, and why would you want to? Beltane, like so many Pagan celebrations, is about having fun while acknowledging the beauty of life.

The Green Men chose to replicate the maypole tradition for our first Beltane celebration, using one of the men as a living pole around whom we danced. It was a mixed success, primarily because we couldn't quite get the whole over-and-under form of the dancing correct, but nonetheless a good time was had by all. We did not, I should say, undertake the more erotic traditions of the sabbat, although of course you certainly could.

To make your own maypole, all you need is a pole of some kind (you can use a stick, a living tree, or, as we did, even a tallish man) and some ribbons, which should be long enough to reach from the top of the pole to the ground and still have about another five feet of length to work with. You can decorate the maypole in any way you like, but it should be bright and cheerful. Then you simply attach the ribbons to the top and let them hang down. For the dancing, have each man take the end of a ribbon in one hand. The dancers face alternating directions, so that half are moving in one direction and half in the other. As music plays or singing commences, the dancers move forward, with half of the men moving clockwise and ducking underneath the raised arms of the other half, who move counterclockwise. The men who ducked under then raise their arms and the other half duck beneath them. By continuing to move around the pole while alternating going under and over, you will wrap the ribbons around the maypole. I can tell you from personal experience that this seldom works smoothly, but the resulting chaos is just as much fun as doing the dance properly, and since Beltane is all about enjoying yourselves, it doesn't matter one bit how your maypole turns out.

After the maypole dance, a perfect celebration for Beltane is a picnic dinner outside, preferably accompanied by a bonfire.

Many Pagans also like to leap over this Beltane fire, either singly or while holding hands with a partner, to bring the power of fire into their lives and relationships. If you incorporate this into your Beltane ritual, the obvious need for care to prevent anyone from turning into a human torch is obvious.

Finally, if you do feel like celebrating the more erotic aspects of Beltane, you're certainly free to do so, either alone or with a partner or partners. As always, keep in mind the purpose of celebrating the sabbats, and undertake your activities with a sense of purpose and intention.

Litha (on or around June 21)

If Yule marks the time when light begins to displace dark, Litha (the summer solstice) marks the time when dark begins to displace light. This is the shortest night of the year, after which the hours of darkness begin to grow longer. It is traditionally a time when the faeries appear to celebrate their queen, Maeve, and to amuse themselves by interfering in the lives of humans. William Shakespeare's delightful *A Midsummer Night's Dream* takes place on Litha and is a perfect example of how this night has historically been thought of.

There is not really a great deal to say about Litha. For me, it is a time of magic and transformation, a night on which you can become anything you want to be, perhaps encountering yourself and others in your life in new and surprising guises. I can think of no better way to celebrate it than by holding a party at which participants become the magical beings they want to be. How? By making masks.

Using masks in ritual and celebrations is a wonderful way to express creativity. Masks can be manifestations of how we see ourselves or would like to see ourselves, and they can also be used to represent characters from stories and legends or deities that might be invoked in ritual.

Masks can be as simple as a paper plate decorated and tied around the head with string, or a paper bag transformed with paints, glued on objects, and anything else you can think of. I have taken a simple Halloween masquerade ball mask (the kind that covers just the eyes and nose) and used hot glue to affix holly leaves all over it, making a Green Man mask that was a big hit at a solstice party. A friend of mine made a fantastic Crone mask by gluing a wild tangle of raw sheep's wool to a plaster cast of her own face. The possibilities are endless.

My own favorite kind of mask to make is the traditional papier-mâché kind. This is very easy to do, and the resulting masks can be decorated in all kinds of ways.

Magical Litha Masks

MATERIALS:

Newspapers
White glue
Warm water
A bucket or bowl to hold the water-glue mixture
Some kind of form to place the papier-mâché on
Gesso (artist's plaster available at most craft stores)
Anything you like for painting or decorating

Note: If you actually want to wear your mask on Midsummer, be sure to start making it well before the day. Masks can take several days to create because of the time it takes the papier-mâché to dry. Also, once you start making masks you might find you want to make more than one.

Step 1: Start by deciding what kind of mask you want to make and what basic form you will need to fashion it. If you're making a simple flat-face mask that will tie on, you can use a paper plate or plastic dish as a form. But most people want to make more complicated things. For example, if you want to make a mask that will fit over your whole head, you need to start with an object that is the approximate size, and preferably larger than, your own head. I have used large balloons and even children's beach balls for large masks. The important thing is to use something that, when the papier-mâché dries, will be easy to remove. Balloons are great because you just pop them and pull the pieces off the papier-mâché. Beach balls are harder, but they work. So do things like plastic jugs. Rubber balls are bad, because the glue adheres to them. You can use forms made of cardboard or sturdy paper, but keep in mind that the base will probably have to stay part of the mask.

Step 2: If you want your mask to have additions like horns, a snout, protruding eyes, a beak, or anything like that, you will need to find appropriately shaped objects to form them on. I have used plastic containers, old bottles, cans, cardboard tubes from toilet paper and paper towels, and even egg cartons to good effect. You can form things like horns out of heavy paper rolled into cone shapes and secured with tape. I once made some wonderful twisting horns out of lengths of foam pipe insulation slipped over spiral forms made of coat hanger wire. Once the papier-mâché dried over them, I slipped the wires out, and the resulting horns were lightweight enough to be glued fairly easily to the main head of the mask.

Step 3: Glue, tape, or otherwise attach your shapes to the main body of your mask. You can tape cups and egg cartons right to balloons if you're careful. You can also make additional features separately and affix them later. For example, while I usually make large eyes or noses directly on the basic form, I generally make horns separately and glue them on when the main head is done.

Step 4: Once you have your basic form, it's time to cover it. Tear the newspaper into strips about 1½ to 2 inches wide and anywhere from 3 to 4 inches long. You might want to make some very small, narrow strips for smaller areas and bigger pieces for larger areas. I find that plain old newspaper works best for papier-mâché, but I have also used heavy brown paper and even tissue paper, although the tissue paper is very hard to use and takes many layers of application to be useful. If you want your paper to be the final finish (the glue will dry clear), then choose something pretty. Otherwise, don't worry about it. You'll be covering up the foundation anyway.

Step 5: Once you have a nice pile of paper strips, it's time to mix the paste. Take a bowl and add some white glue, maybe four or five tablespoons to start. Then add about twice that amount in warm water. Mix it well, so that you have a thin, white paste. The paste should be sticky, but not lumpy and not overly runny. It's not hard to make the paste, so use your judgment about how much water to add. You'll be surprised how little paste you actually use for an average-sized mask, so don't go crazy and use the whole bottle of glue. I usually use about a fourth of a bottle per mask.

Step 6: Once you have your strips and paste, the rest is easy. Dip a strip of paper into the paste. Don't let it sit in the paste, or it will become soggy. Just run it through the paste so that both sides are covered. Let the excess drip off, or run it through your fingers to remove extra paste.

Now place the strip on your mask form, smoothing it on with your fingers. Start at any point you like, but remember that you might need to hold the mask in your hand at some point while working on it, so work accordingly so that the point you hold is the last point you cover.

Work over the entire mask, applying pieces of pasted paper. Be sure to overlap edges, as this forms a more sturdy base. And don't worry about making every edge perfect. Excess paper can be easily cut away when the mask dries. Use the same technique to make horns, ears, snouts, and so on.

Step 7: Once the whole mask is covered, let it dry. This can take from a few hours to overnight, depending on how much paste you used, how heavily you applied the strips, and what the conditions of the room are.

Step 8: When the mask is dry to the touch, apply a second layer of strips. Continue this process of drying and applying strips until the mask is very sturdy. I generally put between four and five layers of paper on a mask. Larger masks will need more layers, as they need the extra support.

If you haven't already attached items such as horns, ears, snouts, and so on, this is the time to do it. Affix them in whatever way is easiest. Then cover the places where these items join the main body of the mask with more strips of paper. This hides seams and also makes the mask as a whole much more solid. Horns especially need extra support, so put two or three layers of pasted paper on to help hold them in place. If your mask is one that fits over your head, make sure that there are holes in the place where you will be looking out from. Sometimes, this place is the actual eyes of the mask. But other times your eye holes will need to be in the nose or even the neck of the papier-mâché head. Try your mask on at different stages to be sure you know where your eye holes will need to go.

When the whole mask is dry, remove the underlying form if you can. If you've used a balloon, simply pop it and pull the pieces off the papier-mâché. Some forms, like plastic containers, often pull away easily, but others, such as beach balls, may have to be cut out. If there are any rough edges, or if you need to reshape the mask so that it fits over your head, simply cut away the excess material with scissors.

Step 9: Now that you have a mask, it's time to cover it with a base coat. I use painter's gesso, which goes on very easily with any paintbrush, covers newsprint and any colors found in the paper, and leaves a smooth, hard finish. If you put enough layers of gesso on, you can even sandpaper it to smooth out any wrinkles that may be there.

It's important to remember here that your mask doesn't have to be perfect. The newspaper will always leave wrinkles and imperfections in the surface of the mask. Don't worry about it. Paint and other decorations will help disguise these things.

Step 10: Once you've applied enough layers of gesso so that you're happy with the finish, decorate your mask in any way you like. Use paints, sequins, pinecones, feathers, shells, flowers, wool, colored paper, or anything else you like. I once made a wonderful Green Man mask out of holly leaves, which I affixed to a basic mask form with a hot glue gun. Let your imagination run wild, and try everything.

Now you're done. If you've made a simple face mask, you will need to be able to tie it on. Make holes in the side of the mask and tie pieces of ribbon through the holes. If you've made a mask that fits over your head, just put it on!

Celebrate Midsummer by dressing up in costumes and your masks. Act out a favorite story or legend, or simply have a big party and enjoy this magical night. Also, you don't have to use your masks only at Midsummer. That's only once a year, but there are plenty of other times when masks would be good additions to your magical work and play. Remember: you create the magic when you put your imagination to work and create something fun and fantastic.

Lammas (August 1)

Also called Lughnasadh (after the Celtic fire god Lugh), this harvest festival celebrated a successful growing season. Traditionally, dolls made out of corn husks were burned in fires, representing the legendary (or perhaps not-so-legendary) sacrifice of the chosen harvest king in exchange for the promise of an equally successful harvest season the following year. I say "perhaps" legendary because there is some evidence that in various cultures specially chosen "kings" were sometimes killed and offered to the gods of the earth in the belief that the blood sacrifice would result in an abundant harvest. Shirley Jackson's infamous short story "The Lottery" is based, at least partially, on this theme of sacrifice for the good of the community, although her story has far more chilling implications, suggesting what happens when people forget the origins of their rituals and distort their meanings.

Witches do not, of course, believe in human sacrifice any more than we believe that we can make such ridiculous bargains with the gods. What we do believe is that making personal sacrifices can aid us in creating the lives that we wish to have. One Lamas ritual I think is particularly effective builds on this idea. You create a doll, preferably out of natural materials like sticks and leaves (or the traditional corn husks if you can find them). As you make the doll—also called a poppet—imagine that you are putting into it all of the parts of you that are standing in the way of you achieving what it is you want: self-doubt, fear, anger, stubbornness, or unhealthy relationships or habits. Imagine that as you tie the sticks, leaves, and husks together that you are binding into the poppet everything you want to rid yourself of.

When your doll is completed, hold it in your hands and talk to it. Tell it what it is you want to rid your life of and why you want to do this. Tell it that you are sacrificing these things so that you can achieve your goals. When you have said everything that you want to say, throw the poppet into a fire and watch it burn. Imagine the smoke taking away all of the obstacles in your life. Commit yourself to pursuing your path now that these things are gone from you.

After performing a ritual such as this, it is a good idea to end it happily, perhaps by partaking in some food with friends, or building a bonfire outside and dancing around it. This is, after all, a celebration, and you want to end your Lammas night with the fire of Lugh burning brightly inside of you.

Mabon (on or about September 21)

As noted in the introduction to the Green Man story about Mabon, this is probably the sabbat about which the least is known. It is the autumn equinox, the day on which dark and light are in balance (much as they are on the vernal equinox of Ostara). At Mabon, however, the year is moving into darkness instead of into light. My favorite representational image of Mabon is of a Half-n-Half or Half Moon cookie, the kind that has one-half frosted in chocolate and one-half frosted in vanilla.

Both sides are delicious by themselves, but somehow having them together on the same cookie makes each side taste even better.

I feel that same way about Mabon. This is my favorite time of year. I love the fall, and to me the autumn equinox represents its arrival. Personally, this tends to be a time of beginnings and endings for me. I often begin projects around this time, and it's frequently at Mabon that I come to see what my work for the coming year is going to be.

In my experience, Mabon rituals tend to be more subdued than some of the others. For me they often involve spending time alone, rather than with a group. Sometimes, I'll spend the evening of Mabon reading a favorite book that reminds me of that part of the year (Jackson's *We Have Always Lived in the Castle*, Tove Jansson's *Moominvalley in November*, and Laird Koenig's *The Little Girl Who Lived Down the Lane* are ones I particularly like). It's my way of celebrating the turning of the Wheel from summer to fall.

Another Mabon ritual I enjoy doing is a variation on the Words of Power ritual suggested for Imbolc. Building on the Words of Power, you can create Phrases of Power. These phrases are challenges that, like the Words of Power, are written on slips of paper and chosen at random. The idea is that whatever phrase you select is your challenge for the coming season. The phrases I have used appear here. You can use them or make your own.

accept a truth
allow yourself
ask a question
show compassion
conceive a new
   project

create a community
fulfill a dream
make others aware
begin again
believe in love
enjoy belonging

build a home
care for your body
celebrate your strengths
accept a challenge
take a chance
create a change
choose a path
make a commitment
celebrate with friends
fulfill a promise
give yourself a present
allow growth
heal an old wound
inspire someone else
invite joy into your life
join a new group
begin your journey
call in joy
spread kindness
laugh at yourself
stand in the light
listen for a call
live with fierce joy
let someone love you
allow the magic
make music
nurture your dearest
   dream
observe your anger
dance for joy
dare to fail
defy expectations
embrace desire

discover a new place
do something new
awaken from a dream
embark on a journey
embrace your difference
emerge into the light
connect with family
feed your hunger
forgive a mistake
make and keep a
   promise
question your beliefs
take time for quiet
enjoy spiritual rebirth
receive a blessing
reclaim your power
recover a lost relationship
reflect on what you want
rejoice in your success
release your fears
remember a kindness
renew a friendship
risk losing it all
search for your
   true self
embrace your
   sexuality
share your life
allow yourself to
   shine
let yourself sing
share your spirit
teach others

open your heart
own your fears
plan for the future
plant a garden
play like a child
praise your loved ones
withdraw and reflect
write your story

thank someone who
  helped
accept touch
trust someone fully
let your path unfold
weave a new circle
welcome a new friend
experience wonder

Samhain (October 31)

As Halloween, this sabbat is known worldwide as a night of magic and mischief making. In reality, Samhain is a very serious sabbat, the Witches' New Year on which the Wheel of the Year comes full circle. In Celtic agrarian communities, Samhain (the name comes from the Celtic word for November) symbolized the end of the year, when the harvest had been taken in and the animals slaughtered to provide food for the winter.

The Halloween traditions that remain today in the form of trick-or-treating and dressing up have their origins in older, more serious, ways of celebrating Samhain. On Samhain, the veil between the world of the everyday and the world we cannot see is at its thinnest. It was thought that on this night the world of humans was visited both by the spirits of the departed and by the inhabitants of the faerie realms, some of whom could be very dangerous.

Out of this belief came several traditions. The jack-o-lantern, for instance, was created as a means of scaring evil or mischievous spirits away from homes. People thought that if they placed grinning jack-o-lanterns in their windows and on their doorsteps they would frighten away anything trying to get in. The giving out of candy or treats symbolized the practice of making offerings to keep the spirits from doing harm. And dressing up served two purposes: originally, it was to confuse the spirits who might be wandering about and, later, it was a way to impersonate these same spirits when humans began to lose their fear of them.

Oddly enough, one of the most vivid images that comes to mind when I think of Samhain comes from a Walt Disney movie. In the section of the film *Fantasia* that begins with Modest Mussorgsky's thrilling *Night on Bald Mountain*, the animators depict a craggy mountain coming to life on Samhain Eve, the rock unfolding to become a towering demon-like figure with blazing eyes, the wings of a bat, and a mouth filled with wicked teeth. As the music plays, the demon summons ghostly skeleton riders, long-haired witches, and all manner of hellish creatures to celebrate with him. The figures of naked women created out of flame dance in his hand as he orchestrates a profane orgy of what I'm sure the film's creators meant to be pure evil.

At the height of the merrymaking, a single note sounds and the demon's triumphant smile fades. Morning has come, and with it darkness is banished. As the demon of the mountain once more becomes rock, a new song is taken up. A group of candle-carrying figures is depicted walking through the woods in the morning light, making their way toward a church in the forest. They sing "Ave Maria," the words of the hymn driving away the last vestiges of darkness.

The symbolism here is clear: The power of Christ has driven the Pagan god away, making the world once again a safe place for those who believe. Although this is not a concept near and dear to my heart, still there is something magical about the pairing of the two pieces of music. And there is another way to look at it as well. November 1 is All Souls Day, a day on which the dead are remembered. If Samhain is the night on which the dead are allowed to roam free, why should not the following day be one of more solemn remembrance? When I watch this portion of *Fantasia*, that is what I think of. The figures in the wood are not banishing darkness as much as they are entering a new season, carrying with them the light inside themselves.

Samhain has, naturally, become *the* sabbat for many witches of both the upper- and lowercased varieties. How you celebrate it is really a matter of choice. One year I attended a typical Halloween party, then went home and spent some time in quiet meditation, thinking about people gone from this world who had in some way influenced me in my work and life. In the first year of the Green Men, we held what turned out to be a deeply moving ritual in which one of the men dressed as the Grim Reaper and chased the rest of us through the house with a scythe to symbolize the inevitability of death.

I am a big believer in combining fun with solemnity, and I really enjoy rituals where (as in that section of *Fantasia*) the sacred and the profane work together. Samhain provides an excellent opportunity to do this, and I encourage you to use your imagination when inventing ways to celebrate this final sabbat of the Wheel of the Year, whether you decide to throw a costume party or spend the night in quiet reflection.

One of the first, and most moving, Samhain rituals I ever attended was held in a beautiful old grange hall in Boston. In the huge central room used for the event, altars had been set up in memory of the dead (including an altar for pets) and we were encouraged to move from one altar to the next throughout the night, talking about loved ones who had passed and remembering the ways they had touched our lives.

One excellent way to celebrate this sabbat is to set up (on your altar, if you have one) a special shrine for a person or people important to you who have passed on. Get a picture or objects connected to the person you want to remember and set them where you can look at them. If you like, you may also add candles and flowers to the shrine, or perhaps food or drinks that the person especially liked. The important thing is to create something that represents the person you want to remember.

On Samhain night, sit and look at the shrine you've created, thinking about the person and what she or he meant to you. If you like, you can close your eyes and imagine the person being there with you, speaking to you. Say whatever you want to say, and see if the person says anything back. Are you really communicating with the spirit of this person? Perhaps. But even if you aren't, you're saying what's in your heart, and you're celebrating that person's role in your life.

You can do this ritual alone, but you can also do it with a group. If you decide to do it with others, have everyone bring pictures or mementos of people they want to remember (it's also perfectly okay to remember animal friends who have died). Go around the room and tell stories about the people you've chosen to remember on Samhain. Share with one another and celebrate the joy these people brought to your lives. Afterward, you might want to have a party to remember and celebrate the joy of living as well.

Because Samhain is considered such a magical night, it is also a good night for divination, for looking into the coming year and seeing what path should be taken and what work should be done. Just as many people make resolutions and plans at the New Year, many Witches like to do the same at Samhain. One way you can look ahead on this night is to do a Tarot card reading for the coming year.

We haven't talked about Tarot cards before in this book because they are not an integral part of the Path of the Green Man. If you are familiar with the cards, however, this ritual may be very meaningful to you.

Take a deck of Tarot cards and shuffle them. Some people

like to shuffle them just as they would a regular deck of cards, while others like to swirl them around in a big pile. Mix the cards up any way you like. Then draw twelve of them, one for each month of the coming year. Again, draw the cards in whatever way appeals to you, either straight from the top of the shuffled deck or randomly from a pile or spread.

Lay the twelve cards out and look at them as if you're looking at the calendar for the coming year. What does each card represent? Do you see any kind of pattern? Remember, Tarot cards represent the general atmosphere surrounding a situation and not necessarily exact events. Try to see what kind of theme runs through the twelve cards you've chosen. Are there lots of cards indicating difficulty? Then perhaps you're going to face a number of challenges during the coming year. Are there lots of cards suggesting relationships with other people? You might find that your year is centered around friends and family.

As with any Tarot reading, don't get too caught up in trying to figure it all out right away. Write down the twelve cards you select and keep the list somewhere where you can refer to it every month. As each new month approaches, look at the card you drew for that month and see if it can help you prepare for what might happen. If you drew a card that suggests your month might be difficult, use that information to be more aware of potential obstacles you might encounter. Don't assume it means something bad will happen; consider it a reminder that you might have to work harder that month.

Similarly, if you drew a really wonderful card for a particular month, don't assume everything will automatically be easy for you that month. The card suggests what *could* happen if you work hard to make that month everything it can be. Use your Samhain Tarot reading as a map for the coming year. If you really pay attention to the cards and try to understand *all* of their possible meanings (and Tarot cards each have many, many meanings), you'll find that your New Year reading will provide you with a lot of helpful information.

A variation on this ritual is depicted in the final story in the Green Man story cycle, in which the Green Man is asked to choose a card from a deck presented to him by the witch Baba Yaga. His chosen card is meant to depict the starting point for his next journey. You may choose to do this as well, selecting one card instead of twelve, and using it as a focal point for your work during the coming season.

As you can see from these examples, how you celebrate a particular sabbat is not really important. What's important is the spirit you bring to your celebration. We celebrate the sabbats because doing so helps us remain close to the cycles of nature and because they give us the opportunity to work on different issues related to the time of year and to the mood of the individual sabbats. When participating in rituals at these times, use your imagination. Apply the ideas of each sabbat to your own life, asking yourself how what's happening in your life is or is not reflective of the sabbat's message. Use these days as times to connect both with the world without and within, and you'll find that your celebrations bring you much joy.

THE DEATH OF JOHN BARLEYCORN
A Story for Lammas

ABOUT LAMMAS

Lammas, like the other three Greater Sabbats of Imbolc, Beltane, and Samhain, is a fire festival. In this case, it is the festival of the Celtic fire god Lugh, a connection more easily seen in the other common name for this sabbat, Lughnasadh (meaning "the commemoration of Lugh"). The name Lammas is itself a variation of Lughomass, a mass in honor of Lugh.

Like any mass, Lammas is, essentially, a celebration, in this case the celebration of the great harvest of summer. It is a time for giving thanks for the bounty of the earth. As such, it was often celebrated with feasts to honor the lord of the fields. Lugh is a sun deity and was seen as the figure responsible for bringing the fields to life. In his honor, the best fruits of the harvest were offered up.

Lammas was also seen as the date of the sacrificial death of a harvest king. In some early societies, the death of a king— either an actual king or a man chosen to represent him—each year was thought to bring good luck to the people. However, it wasn't practical to go offing kings once a summer. To symbolize this sacrifice, cakes were baked in the shape of men and broken open in Lammas rituals. Made of grains, they were of the earth, and when eaten they sustained the celebrants. Thus was the king sacrificed and born again, and no one was any worse for it.

A popular figure at Lammas rituals was John Barleycorn, who appeared in the form of one of these cakes or, more usually, as a figure made of barley and corn stalks whose body was sometimes filled with the fruits of the harvest. This figure represented both the successful harvest and the god who made it possible, and when the John was burned it was both the symbolic sacrifice of the king and an offering to the god of the fields in exchange for another bountiful harvest the next year.

Since few of us live in agrarian societies now, this story focuses on what other gifts of the harvest we might have to give to Lugh in thanks for what we have reaped during the year. As you think about your own Lammas ritual, think about the special gifts you have that you can share, both with Lugh and the other deities, and with those who come to your table.

THE SUMMER RIPENED as the sun drew the fields up into its arms, filling the valley with seas of barley and corn. As the Green Man walked through the days, he felt as if the entire world was lit with gold. His face was brown from long afternoons spent walking the paths of his home, and his head was filled with thoughts of joy. At night he sat on a hill covered with stars and watched the comings and goings of the constellations while he remembered all he had learned during the year and felt the lingering touch of the golden day on his skin.

These things he turned into stories, poems, and songs, which he shared with the moon and the trees. Soon others, hearing his words, also came to listen. They were the inhabitants of the woods, fields, hills, and streams. Some stayed in the shadows, never seen, while others made themselves known, gathering around to hear his tales. The Green Man told stories to all who came to hear him. He told them of the Horned One and of Brigid's fire. He told them how the Child of Light was born from Gaia's egg and of the night when men made love with one another in the fields of Pan. He told them of the Oak King's death and the Holly King's birth, and sometimes he wore the mask he made in Maeve's wood and looked out at the night with eyes that were only half his.

On one such night, as he sang again of the Oak King and his gift of death, there came a new listener. He was a man, or at least he inhabited the form of a man. He walked up the hill where the Green Man sat telling his story and he laid down in the grass nearby. He listened while the Green Man finished his tale, and when he spoke his voice was like the wind through the fields.

"It is a rare gift you give," he said. "I can see you have traveled far during this year. But tell me, what comes after the story of the Oak King and the Holly King?"

The Green Man sat quietly for some time, listening to the

sounds of the night. The stranger had asked the question that he, too, had been hoping to find an answer to. He had indeed journeyed far. He had received many gifts and learned much about the world and about himself. His eyes had been opened, and his heart had followed gladly after. Now he found himself at the fullness of summer and of his year, and he knew not where to go next.

"What comes next has not been revealed to me," he told the stranger, his voice betraying something of the sadness he felt at hearing his own words.

The man sat up, his form dark against the light of the moon. "The harvest comes soon," he said. "The time of gathering in."

"You are a farmer?" the Green Man asked.

The man laughed. "Let us say that the gifts of the fields interest me," he said. "Especially at this time of the year."

"It is almost the night of John Barleycorn," the Green Man said. "I had almost forgotten."

"Indeed it is," the stranger said. "The people will be giving their best to him in thanks for the harvest. Tell me, friend, what do you have for Barleycorn this year?"

"The same as last," said the Green Man. "The grain from my field and the bounty of my garden."

"Is that all?" asked the man.

The Green Man was puzzled. He had offered these things in thanks to the god of the fields each year, and each year had been blessed again with a rich harvest.

"Are they not enough?" he asked.

The man's eyes glittered in the night. "I think you have something much more precious to give," he said.

"I have many things," said the Green Man, thinking of his home and valley. "But none worthy of a god."

"It is often surprising what the gods find worthy," said the man, standing up.

"You are going?" asked the Green Man. He was enjoying the stranger's company, even if his words were puzzling, and was sorry to see him go so soon.

"I have other business to attend to this night," said the man. "But I will return tomorrow to hear another story."

He walked away into the darkness, and the Green Man sat alone for some time afterward. He had told all of his stories many times over and knew them all by heart. He wanted to create something new for the stranger, some story no one had yet heard from him. He thought for a long time before returning to his home and bed, and even as he began to dream his mind sought out new words to share with the stranger on the hill.

The next day the Green Man walked the valley, winding among the towering corn and the nodding heads of barley, in search of a story. He saw men gathering up the grain into thick bunches, and he watched as women tossed the newly threshed barley into the air on sheets of white muslin, laughing as the wind carried away the chaff and they were left with handfuls of the rich, brown seeds.

In a field not far from the river he came across a group of children. They were collecting the discarded leaves and silk from the corn stalks where the men had passed, and their hands were filled with the green and golden treasure. Several of them had already begun winding the leaves into thick bunches, which they tied with rough twine. These they placed in a pile.

"We have almost enough for the John," said one, wiping her brow and smiling.

The others joined her with the last armfuls of corn, and they all helped to bind the leaves into limbs, which they fastened together with more twine. Soon, they had the rough shape of a man, his arms and legs sticking out as though he were embracing the whole of the world. His head they made of a circle of leaves, the silk from the corn forming his hair. This they affixed to the body, and then they stood the figure upright.

"John Barleycorn," said the girl who had called the others to work. "The finest John I have ever seen in all the valley."

The others cheered. They held hands and danced around the figure happily, calling out his name in their bright, happy voices. Then, as if by some unspoken agreement, they collapsed in gales of high, rolling laughter.

The Green Man left them there with their John. He knew that all over the valley others were making similar corn figures, all of which would be set in places of honor on Lammas Eve. It was their way of celebrating the harvest and thanking the god for another year of plenty. Around the John they would set the best of their harvests, gifts returned to he who walked the rows and blessed them with his touch. They would offer their gifts with fire and smoke, sending their prayers and thanks into the late summer sky.

That night the Green Man returned to his hill and sat under a tree. As the moon crept over the hill, it brought with it the stranger of the night before. Once more he came and sat by the Green Man.

"I did not know if you would come," said the Green Man.

"I had much business in the valley today," the man said. "I am weary. But I came to see what story you have for me to-night."

The Green Man closed his eyes and thought of the children he had seen that afternoon. He told the stranger about how he had watched their game, had watched John Barleycorn be born. He described their busy hands and their faces flushed with work and joy. He told the man the song they sang. Then he told him about his own childhood and about the Johns he had made. He talked of forming the arms and legs from stalks of corn and of fashioning the head from leaves, cobs, and, once, an early pumpkin.

As he talked, the Green Man found himself remembering more and more. Soon, he was speaking about the feel of corn silk in his hands and the smell of earth and fresh-cut barley. He recalled the thrill of seeing the completed John standing before him, beautiful and terrible in its form so much that of a man yet also silent and godlike. He thought of a night, long ago, when he crept from the house of his parents to stand in the field on the night before Lammas Eve. There he had sat at the feet of the John, which stood waiting to fulfill its purpose, and talked. He talked of the seasons, the stars, and his fears. He talked about the happiness he felt when his hands were in the earth or when he dove, reckless, into deep pools of water. He talked of the warmth of the sun and the delicious cold of winter. He talked until dawn slid over the hills, and then he said good-bye to the John and returned to his own bed, where his mother found him in the morning and wondered why he was so late in coming to breakfast.

"I have not thought of that night in many years," the Green Man told the stranger when he was done. "The memory is a good one, and I am glad to have it back."

"And I am thankful to have shared it with you," said the stranger. "It makes staying up with the night worth the price I will pay in sleep."

Again he stood and walked into the dark, saying as he left, "I will come tomorrow."

The Green Man stayed a while longer, thinking of child-hood and magic. Then he, too, walked home and slept. He dreamed that night of John Barleycorn and of being a boy of seven summers, and this time when he had finished telling the John his stories, he heard a voice say to him, "Your gift is well chosen, young one."

The next day the Green Man again ventured out into the valley. This time he walked in a different direction, following a road that led through land that had been farmed since before imagining. As he neared the farm that had been born from this rich land, he saw that the windows had been hung with flowers. The women and men of the place went about preparing for the next day, for Lammas Eve. In the oldest of the fields, two great shire horses were pulling a wagon piled high with corn, barley, and other fruits of the harvest. Their great hooves brought up clouds of dust around their legs as they moved, snorting, with their driver urging them on.

The Green Man stood on the road and watched as the horses stopped in the very center of the field. There, a great figure was being erected by the men of the farm. It was a John, but much larger than that created by the children. This John stood three times the height of a man. His limbs were made from wood, his body from a cage formed of branches and corn stalks. Into this cage were placed the things from the wagon, the ripest barley and the most golden ears of corn, the vegetables from the garden and the flowers from the field. The men took them and affixed them to the John wherever they would go, until he was decorated all around with their gifts.

When they were done, all that remained to be added was the head. The Green Man knew that this they would do on the morrow, on Lammas Eve, as those who were given life by the farm gathered round and sang John Barleycorn into being before lighting the fire that would send their gifts nightward. But for now, the men all drew mugs of beer from a keg that sat at the feet of the John and toasted his health. Some of the beer they drank, and some they poured on the ground to nourish it. Then they climbed into the wagon and the horses turned their heads toward the barn.

Later, as the Green Man told the stranger of these things

while they sat together under the late summer sky, he remembered how he had loved, as a boy, to watch the burning of the John. It was both terrifying and enchanting to watch the wood crackle with life as the flames crept up and up, enfolding the John in its arms. The first time he had seen it he had cried, fearing that it would hurt the John. Then his father had lifted him up in strong arms and sat him on his shoulders.

"The fire harms him not at all," he had told his son in his quiet way. "He is a child of Lugh, a child of the fire and the sun. He goes now to his father, carrying with him our prayers and our thanks. Do not cry for him. Instead, sing him on his way."

And then they had sung, the people of the valley, their voices joining together and rising with the smoke. And as he told the stranger of their singing, the Green Man remembered words he thought he had long forgotten.

> *Field from Earth and rain from Water,*
> *wind from Air and flame from Fire.*
> *In John Barleycorn we join thee,*
> *formed from branch and leaf and briar.*
>
> *Summer's ending brings the darkness,*
> *as the Wheel turns once more.*
> *Winter's touch will end the growing,*
> *but our barns are filled with stores.*
>
> *Now we offer thanks and blessings,*
> *to the Lord of farm and vale,*
> *in the smoke that rises skyward,*
> *in our gifts of food and ale.*
>
> *Barleycorn burns bright this Lammas,*
> *sacrificed with joy and love.*

In the spring he once more rises,
wakened by the sun above.

"Those are words I have not heard sung in many a year," the stranger said when the Green Man had finished.

"I've heard none sing it since the passing of my father," said the Green Man. "Now they sing new songs, ones of their own."

"But you have given the old one life again," said the man. "There is magic in that."

He stood to go, and the Green Man called to him. "Tomorrow is Lamas Eve," he said. "Will you come, or do you have business of your own?"

"I will come," he said simply and was gone.

That night when the Green Man returned home, he sat for a long while at his table. He had before him a pile of corn husks, taken from his fields. On these he wrote stories. He wrote about his journey of the year. He wrote about the things he had seen, heard, and dreamed. He wrote them in snatches of poems and in lines from songs. He wrote them as if he were telling stories to the stranger, and the more he wrote, the more alive he felt.

He wrote all through the next day and into the afternoon, and then he put down his pen and gathered up the corn husks. These he took into the field, where he fashioned them into the figure of John Barleycorn, winding the leaves around the branches and stalks he fastened together.

When he was finished, it was dusk. He went into his house and gathered up the best of his harvest, filling his bags with vegetables, breads, meats, and cheeses. He took up a skin of wine and one of ale, and he slung them on his back. Then he picked up his John and carried him up the hill.

There, he laid out a feast at the feet of John Barleycorn, and then he sat beneath the tree and waited. As night drew on, he saw flickers of light across the valley, and he knew that others were burning their Johns. He saw a larger fire burning some way off, and he knew that at the oldest farm the people were singing and dancing as they offered up their gifts.

He waited for the stranger, but the stranger did not come. Finally, when midnight was drawing on, the Green Man could wait no longer. Pouring some of the wine into a cup, he addressed the John.

"To John Barleycorn," he said, "may he return next year in as good health as he has enjoyed this season."

He drank deeply, then poured some of the wine onto the ground around the John's feet. He did the same with the ale, also offering some to the ground. Then he lit the husks of the figure's feet and watched as the flames grew brighter.

"A fine John you have there," said the stranger as he came out of the darkness.

"Not the biggest, nor the most handsome," said the Green Man, happy to see his friend, "but he was made with love. I am sorry to have started without you. I'm afraid you missed the toast."

"That I did not," said the man. "And I am still in time for the feast."

"But that is for the John," he said. "And through him the Lord of the harvest. It is my gift to him."

"Your stories were the only gift I needed this Lammas," said the stranger. "They are more precious to me than any breads or ale, and much more filling. They will sustain me during the long winter, as your memories of this season and of seasons past will sustain you as long as you share them with all who come to listen. This food here we will eat together, in friendship, as you should eat with all who join as friends at your table."

And then the Green Man knew who his companion of the

previous nights truly was. He also knew that in harvesting his stories, and the stories of others, he had fed himself and all those who listened to him. In astonishment, he sat and shared his food with Lugh, watching as the Lammas fires burned in the valley and his offering of words was turned into smoke that filled the sky.

Developing a Practice

Now that we've looked at the basic tenets underlying Wiccan philosophy (the Rede and Law of Three), examined Wiccan theology (the concept of deity), discussed the nature of magic, and laid out the Wheel of the Year, it's time to talk about how you put all of these things together to create a coherent practice that you can express and explore on a daily basis. In other words, how you walk the Path of the Green Man.

I've said before that the only thing you need to participate in *any* spiritual tradition is your mind. The physical trappings—places of worship, sacred texts, and the odds and ends that often accompany ceremonial worship—are just add-ons. They're the things that aid us (and sometimes hinder us) in our spiritual work, but they are not the work itself.

You begin walking the Green Man's path by asking yourself why you're attracted to this kind of spirituality. What is it about Paganism, or Witchcraft, that speaks to you? Is it just something that sounds cool to do, or something you can imagine shocking your friends and family with? If so, then your heart probably isn't in the right place for this path to be of much use for you. If, however, your interest in Pagan spirituality comes from a genuine interest in discovering how it might help you achieve a fuller, more satisfying life, then that's a good beginning.

I encourage anyone interested in a spiritual tradition—Pagan or otherwise—to begin by making a list of what is important in a spiritual tradition. What do you really believe about things like deity and the connection between humanity and divinity? What do you feel the role of spirituality in your life is? What things in your life would you like your spiritual practice to help you address? The more you understand yourself and what you're looking for, the more you're going to get out of your involvement in a spiritual journey.

Once you've decided to begin your journey, you start with the first step on the path. This means establishing a mind-set conducive to doing spiritual work. I recommend committing yourself to exploring the Path of the Green Man for a set time—a month or (if you're feeling particularly witchy and the timing is right) one full cycle of the moon from new to new or full to full. Committing yourself in this way establishes intention and creates a solid mental base on which to build. Tell yourself that for the time period you've selected, you're going to walk the path as fully as you can, even if it becomes difficult. Mark your start and end dates on a calendar.

I also strongly suggest keeping some sort of a journal of your journey. This doesn't have to be anything fancy. You can write down your daily thoughts in a notebook if you like or simply type them up in a computer file. The purpose isn't to create some literary masterpiece, it's to provide you with some record of your progress that you can refer to as you go along.

Speaking from personal experience, I can tell you that I hate keeping journals. But in the beginning of my practice I forced myself to keep one, and I'm glad that I did. Now, I sometimes refer back to it to remember what I was doing at a particular time in my life and to keep track of the different rituals I've tried and how they did or did not work. Sometimes, I'm horribly embarrassed by myself, but more often than not this is a useful exercise. Much of this book, in fact, is drawn from the journal I kept during my first year of intense study, and rereading it I remembered a lot of things I would otherwise have forgotten.

Now that you've committed yourself to walking the Path of the Green Man for however long you've chosen, I recommend finding a place where you can be alone to do your work. This could be your bedroom, a backyard, a park, a beach—any place where you feel comfortable and where you can be reasonably sure you won't be disturbed. It should be a place where you feel comfortable and safe, and hopefully a place that makes you feel happy. Again, this all contributes to the mood of your work and will affect how you approach your spiritual undertakings.

If possible, choose a time of day that is available to you on a regular basis for at least half an hour. Like your chosen spot for your spiritual work, the time you select should be one during which you feel relaxed and unhurried. The half-hour before rushing off to work or class is not ideal. Nor is the half-hour before you throw yourself into bed, exhausted from a long day. Preferably, this will be a time when there are no or few potential demands on you, when your thoughts can be on what you're doing and not on other business.

Once you've chosen your place and time of practice, you can begin. What follows is a four-week plan that can be used for an initial period of study. Depending on the length of time you've chosen to work for, you can adapt this schedule as necessary.

Week 1

Start off by simply sitting in your chosen spot and relaxing. Wear comfortable clothes. Make your space as peaceful as possible, turning off harsh lights and telephones and removing other potential distractions (including pets, who seem to be immediately drawn to you when you begin this exercise). If it helps you relax, light candles or incense. However, I don't suggest playing music, because no matter how soothing or lovely it is, it occupies a portion of your thoughts and distracts from what you're doing.

The primary goal of this exercise is to get your mind into a state where you're open to the work you're going to do. This is best done by practicing the Spell to Open the Door found in chapter 5. This is really the most basic exercise for creating a positive atmosphere and for beginning to work with your inner energies and intentions.

Read over the Spell to Open the Door until you can visualize it in your mind. For the first week do this exercise every day. Try to maintain your meditative state for half an hour. It's okay if your thoughts wander a bit, as I can almost guarantee you they will. Keep with it as best you can. The most important thing right now is establishing in your mind your personal "place of power," the place you imagine yourself when you close your eyes to meditate.

For some people, this place will be the physical location they're sitting in. For others, it will be someplace completely different. Although I generally perform this exercise indoors, my personal place is a clearing in a forest (I like to think it's the Horned God's wood) where tall fir trees form a large circle around me and I can see the sky above me. This image came to me the first time I did the Spell to Open the Door, and it's remained with me ever since. I go to this place in my mind when

I need to calm and center myself. Sometimes, I can even tell how I'm feeling at the time by how the circle looks when I put myself there, by whether it's night or day, summer or winter, quiet or filled with the noises of the forest.

More recently, another special place has come to me. This one is an underwater kelp forest, like the ones I frequently scuba dive in here in California. Like my woodland clearing, this circle is surrounded by towering kelp plants, their fronds forming a canopy overhead with the sun filtering down through them. Graceful leopard sharks, shy harbor seals, and mischievous sea lions dart in and out of this forest as I sit among them, surrounded by the sea that is so important in my life. It doesn't matter that in the real world without scuba equipment I couldn't be sitting there; in my meditations I can breathe easily all on my own.

Wherever your place is, imagine it in as much detail as you can. What about it do you find appealing? What does it look, smell, and feel like? Remember, it doesn't matter where your place is, only that it's a place you love. You can imagine a space station orbiting Jupiter, a cliff overlooking the sea, or the right-field bleachers at Fenway Park. As long as you feel comfortable there, this is your place of power. Whether or not it exists in the real world is immaterial.

Each time you sit down to begin your practice (and I do suggest that you sit, preferably on the floor, but in a chair if you need to) train your mind to go to this special place. Prod it along until the image of your place comes easily and fully developed. When it does, move on to the second part of the Spell to Open the Door by practicing drawing energy up from this place of yours so that it fills your body.

You may find you have unexpected responses to this exercise. You may feel elated and peaceful, but you may also find yourself feeling frightened or just plain ridiculous. These are all natural reactions to opening up your mind and heart to spiritual work. However you feel, take note of it but don't let it overwhelm you, even if the feeling is a pleasant one. You want to be very conscious of the emotions this work evokes in you. You might find that initially you have a very hard time with the exercise. Don't give up. Keep at it, and I can almost guarantee you that within a short time you'll find yourself looking forward to your visits to your magical place and will find yourself going there more and more easily. Soon, this will become second nature to you. I've gone to my magical place on airplanes, in cars, and anywhere else I've had need to.

During this first week, in conjunction with the meditative work you do, start paying more attention to the world around you. By this I mean be conscious of the physical natural world and how you feel in it, but also the way in which you interact with the world on a daily basis. Examine your responses to people and situations and your feelings about being in certain places. In particular, start thinking about how the ways you act and think might be affecting the rest of the world. If you become angry at someone, for example, try to see how your response to this person or to the situation that has angered you might set off a chain of events that results in negative responses. Think of different ways you could react that might bring about a different result.

My favorite situations to use for this activity involve driving. I don't like to drive, and I particularly don't like to drive on roads with people who drive badly, which seems to be pretty much anywhere. I find myself getting furiously angry with people who don't signal, who don't stop properly at stop signs, or who drive forty-five miles per hour in the fast lane on the freeway. As anyone who has ever ridden in a car with me will attest, I find this kind of behavior completely unacceptable, and dealing with it will put me in a foul mood almost instantly.

As my partner says to me on a regular basis, "I hope yelling at that car is making *you* feel better, because it's just giving me a headache." Well, it is sort of making me feel better, but not really. I'm angry because I feel the other driver is being selfish and not playing by the rules that others of us have agreed to. I resent that people are allowed to get away with this kind of behavior, but mostly I'm angry because I feel that bad driving comes from being completely unaware of other people and your affect on them. If you were genuinely concerned with the well-being of others, wouldn't you *want* to let them know when you're going to turn left? Wouldn't you want to not hold them back by driving too slowly in the wrong lane?

Now, I may be completely justified in these feelings (as I often tell myself while muttering at someone doing something stupid on the road), but does getting angry at everyone who does something stupid help anything? Sadly, no. So what I try to do now when I get angry at someone while I'm driving is to remind myself that this is not exactly a matter of cosmic importance. I can go around someone who's driving too slowly. I can ignore the jerk who insists on switching from lane to lane just to get ahead of one more car. I can focus on what I am doing and feeling, and by doing this I can (sometimes) turn these negative, angry feelings into more positive ones.

I should admit that I'm not really big on "opportunities for growth" as we call them here in California. I recognize their usefulness, and the importance of taking them, but I frequently do it resentfully. Like most people, I don't like to be reminded that I haven't become the fully enlightened being I picture myself as when I'm secretly playing cosmic rock star in my mind. But if there's one thing I'm sure of, it's that the universe will always be there to remind you when you've gotten too big for your britches.

During your first week, look for these opportunities.

They're sure to come up. You can also make them happen. For example, pick something in your life—the food you eat or the clothes you wear—and really think about them. Think about where they come from, who grows them or makes them, and how your purchasing these things affects other people.

Food is an excellent one to begin with. I never thought much about where my food came from until I started driving regularly through a farming area near my home. Suddenly, I started noticing fields of vegetables. Then I started noticing the women and men planting and picking the vegetables and putting them into boxes, boxes I often see at the big supermarket I frequent. I started thinking about these women and men and asking myself what kind of lives they have. What do they want from life? What kinds of dreams do they have? How do they feel about getting up at dawn to pick artichokes, or standing in the hot sun throwing radishes and corn into boxes so that people with more money can buy them?

Because things like food are so readily available to us, we often forget that there are people behind them, people with hopes and fears, people who feel good and bad about their lives, people who have dreams for themselves and their children. How does my attitude toward the food I buy and eat affect these people? How am I changing—for good or for bad—the way they live?

This is a lot to attach to a carrot or a potato, but these are valid questions. When a friend of mine returned from a scuba diving trip to Honduras, she told me how she had learned that many of the men and boys along the Mosquito Coast are badly crippled as a result of having decompression illness (which affects, among other things, the body's neurological systems) from diving to catch lobsters that are sold to a very popular and successful chain of American seafood restaurants. While this chain advertises its amazing bargains on lobster dinners, few customers know that their delicious deals are made possible by boys as young as four or five who are paid almost nothing to make dive after dive, with disastrous results (brain damage, paralysis, and ruptured lungs are some of the byproducts). Is a cheap lobster really worth the price of a person's ability to walk or his life? No, of course it's not. But unless we ask ourselves how actions we often take for granted—things as simple as buying groceries or going out to dinner—might be affecting the larger world, we won't change our behaviors.

Use this first week to start looking for these connections in your daily life. Again, don't feel you have to map out every single connection between you and everything else on the planet. Just start to become more aware than you might have been about your place in the larger picture.

Week 2

In the second week of your journey, you can add a new meditation to your daily practice. This time when you sit down in your chosen location, instead of bringing to mind your personal magical spot, imagine yourself standing at the entrance to an ancient forest. Picture a path before you, stretching away into the trees. It doesn't matter if the wood you see is in a particular season or place. Just let the image of a wood come to you, in whatever form it takes.

This is the home of the Horned God, the lord of the forest and the teacher of the Green Man. You are going to journey into the forest to find the Horned God and speak to him. You have become the Green Man setting out on his journey of self-discovery.

Imagine yourself walking through the wood. Take note of what kinds of trees you're walking through, what season it is, and what animals and plants you see around you. As with all of this meditative work, there's no right or wrong way to do this exercise. Just let your mind take over and show you where you are.

Continue to walk through the wood until you come to a clearing. You may come directly to this clearing, or you may find yourself walking a long way through other clearings, along streams, or up steep hills. Wherever the path takes you, keep going until you come to the clearing.

When you reach it, step inside. You will find the Horned God waiting for you. What does he look like? How does seeing him make you feel? Note your responses to seeing him. None of them are wrong. There's no one way for the Horned God to look, no one way that seeing him will affect you. You may feel relieved, excited, sad, frightened, or even aroused.

Go to the Horned God and greet him in a way that seems fitting. See how he responds to you, if he speaks, gestures, or does nothing. Sit before him and talk to him. Tell him why you have come to his wood. Tell him your hopes and fears about walking the Path of the Green Man. See if he has anything to say to you. If he does, listen carefully. If he doesn't, that's fine too.

Don't worry about whether or not you're "making all this up." That's not the point. The point is that you're bringing to life the feelings you have about undertaking a spiritual journey. This meditation is your opportunity to come face to face with the Horned God, the one around whom the Path of the Green Man was created. Experience him however you experience him.

When you are done talking with the Horned God, thank him for spending time with you and leave. Walk back along the path you traveled to reach him until you come to the entrance to the wood. You may be surprised to discover that the path back looks and feels different from the path that brought you here. If it is, pay attention to the differences. When you arrive at the entrance to the forest, your meditation is over.

Like you did in week 1, practice this meditation each day for the second week. Each time may be the same, or it may be completely different. The Horned God may appear differently every time. He may say things or ask questions of you. Again, don't worry about where the experience is coming from or whether the Horned God "really" exists or doesn't.

This exercise is accomplishing two things. First, it's helping you see what you hope to get out of walking the Path of the Green Man. By conversing with the Horned God, you're giving voice to things you may or may not have realized about what you're looking for, what you're afraid of, and what gifts you possess that will aid you in your journey.

Second, you are beginning to build an image of the Horned God in your mind. As the teacher of the Green Man, the Horned God will become very important to your magical and spiritual work. How you see him will tell you a great deal about yourself and how you see your spiritual journey. Is he a stern figure or a reassuring one? Is he someone you find sexually appealing? Is he someone you find intimidating? Probably, he'll be a little of all these things.

Keeping your image of the Horned God in your head, start searching for other images of gods and the Green Man in history. Look up information about Cernunos, Pan, and other forest deities. Explore Green Man imagery and stories, much of which is readily available in reference books or online. See how you relate to these images and stories. If you're feeling particularly creative, draw your own images based on your interactions with the Horned God, or write a story or poem about your experience.

What you're doing here is strengthening your connection to the central figures of Green Man spirituality. If you are a visual person, it helps to have such images around you. For example, I like to collect various pieces of artwork (particularly statues) that represent, to me, the spirit of the Horned God. Not that my house is filled with these things, but I do have several out where I can see them and be reminded of the path I've chosen to walk and the figure I see as being most representative of that path. I have small statues of Cernunos and Pan, for example, and on my desk there is a tiny Mexican Day of the Dead figure I picked up on a dive trip to Cozumel—a skeleton shaman holding a rattle in each hand and wearing a stag's head mask. Not only does looking at what I see as an incarnation of the Horned God remind me of a wonderful trip I took but he also reminds me of the cycles of life and death and the power of magic.

If you continue to follow the Path of the Green Man, the Horned God is going to become a powerful symbol for you as well. Also, you will come to see yourself as the Green Man journeying through his woods. Start now to work with these images, and you will discover that they appear over and over again in the work that you do.

Week 3

Beginning with week three of your journey, continue doing the Spell to Open the Door and Horned God meditations. In addition, start to incorporate the Wheel of the Year into your daily practice. If you are undertaking your month of study during a time when one of the eight sabbats is being celebrated, focus your attention on that sabbat. If Yule falls during your month of study, for example, plan a small Yule celebration to mark the occasion. This doesn't have to be a major undertaking. Simply come up with a way to mark this longest night of the year. Use any of the suggestions found in chapter 6 or make up your own.

Just as it's important for you to connect with the Horned God and with your personal place of power, it's important that you begin establishing ways to mark the turning of the Wheel of the Year. The sooner you begin to celebrate the changing seasons and the different cycles of nature, the sooner you will begin to incorporate what these changes represent in your life.

When I began studying Wicca, I got *really* into the whole Wheel of the Year thing. I made an altar on which I placed different decorations for each sabbat. I was just the tiniest bit compulsive about what color the altar cloths were, what kind of candles I put there, and what symbols of the season I used. I was so into it all that I pretty much ignored what the whole point of observing the sabbats was.

This is easy to do, which is why, at least at the beginning, I encourage you to keep the props to a minimum. If it helps you to make an altar and decorate it with symbols of the seasons, or with images of the Green Man and/or the Horned God, by all means do so, but keep in mind that these things are only decorations. The real magic comes from understanding what the sabbats mean to you.

If no sabbats occur during your month of initial study, don't worry. They are just the most obvious dates on which to connect to the Wheel. But you don't need a sabbat to celebrate your spirituality, just as Christians don't need Easter or Christmas to celebrate theirs. The Wheel keeps turning whether it's a sabbat or not, and every day is an opportunity to experience the constant change of the natural world.

If you have no sabbat to focus on, focus on the time of year. If it's fall, use your meditation times to think about how the season makes you feel, what thoughts it brings up in your mind and what the fall months make you feel like doing or not doing. Look for patterns in your life that are related to the seasons. Do the traditional "family holidays" of a particular season affect your mood? Do you tend to begin or end relationships at certain times of the year? When is your birthday, and do you feel any special connection to the season in which it falls?

These may all seem like questions totally unrelated to your spirituality, but they might not be as far removed as you think. Many of us are keenly aware of how our outlook on life changes depending on the season, the weather, and the activities associated with different times of the year. For example, many years ago I came to the realization that while I love fall, the winter holiday season made me incredibly tense. Partially, this had to do with the expectations associated with gift-giving, family, and the usual holiday stress. But the more I examined my feelings about this time of year, I saw that my irritability also grew from a feeling that the spiritual meaning of the season—whether in Pagan or Christian traditions—was too often buried under rampant commercialization. Because I felt so rushed during the winter months, I felt as if I never got to properly experience what the various holidays meant to me.

As a result, I decided to more or less stop doing everything I'd been doing to prepare for the holidays. I stopped buying so many gifts and instead decided that every year I would choose an organization to donate money to and send everyone on my gift list a card letting them know to whom the money had gone. I did away with the list of hundreds of people I felt obligated to send Christmas cards to, paring it down to people I really wanted to remain in contact with and choosing to send cards with a Yule message instead of the usual Santas and reindeer. In short, I reclaimed Yule for myself, and as a result I now look forward to the holiday season in ways I wasn't able to for many years.

This is a fairly dramatic example of how focusing on the meaning of the sabbats changed how I dealt with one of them. You certainly don't have to follow my lead on this one. Your way of connecting with whatever point the Wheel is at in the year may be planting bulbs to bloom in the spring or engaging in an outdoor activity associated with the season. One year for Litha I planned a scuba diving outing so that I could be in my favorite element—water—on the sabbat. It was simply a fun way to connect with nature on a day that is special to me as a Green Man. (This year, by the way, I'm celebrating Mabon by diving with my beloved Great White sharks—an activity that for many reasons seems particularly appropriate to a day devoted to the mingling of light and dark.)

How you choose to celebrate the season you find yourself in is a matter of personal taste. You may do it in small, private ways, or you may choose to do something on a grander scale (a Samhain party, perhaps). The important thing is that you start thinking of the year in terms of cycles, as the constantly turning Wheel that symbolizes the spiritual path you've dedicated yourself to.

Week 4

Ready for a little magic? Don't worry, you're just going to do a little bit in this fourth week. In fact, this magic is really just an extension of some you've been doing all along. Remember how you've been practicing visualizing your place of power? And remember how you've been working with drawing energy up from the earth? Now you're going to put these things to-gether and do what we call casting a circle.

Casting a circle means creating sacred/magical space in which to perform a ritual or practice magic. You'll frequently hear Wiccans refer to belonging to a circle (such as the Green Men circle) or to doing work within a circle. What they're re-ferring to is this sacred space. The circle is a basic Wiccan sym-bol (think the Wheel of the Year) symbolizing completeness and cycles. We often refer to the groups we work with as circles, and we often refer to the space in which we work as a circle.

There are many, many ways to cast a circle. The one you're going to work with this week involves bringing energy into yourself by performing the Spell to Open the Door and then sending that energy out to form a circle around yourself. The idea is that within the circle you form you remain safe and pro-tected. From what? Well, that depends who you ask. There are some people who believe that a circle prevents unwanted ener-gies or presences from interfering with what is taking place within the circle. In my experience, the purpose of a circle is most often to provide a space in which the energy you raise within yourself is focused. It's like your place of power but with an added boost of energy. If it were a laundry detergent, its box would probably read: NOW WITH 50% MORE MAGIC!

These are finer points of magical work that can be more fully explored as your study of the path deepens. At this stage, you're just interested in casting a simple circle in which to med-itate. So what do you do? Go through all the steps of the Spell to Open the Door, stopping at the point when you feel yourself filled with light (step 6).

Now you want to send that energy out to create the circle. The easiest way, in my experience, is to hold your hands out and visualize the energy flowing out of your fingertips and forming a circle of blazing light around you. This light may take many forms: flames that leap up to the ceiling, a simple golden ring, or maybe twinkling multicolored lights. You can visualize whatever you like. The point is, this is *your* space. It can look like whatever you want it to look like.

When you can visualize the circle surrounding you, hold this image in your head and tell yourself that you are creating sacred space in which to work. Imagine the circle you've created as a bubble filled with warmth and light that surrounds you as you work.

For some of you, this may be getting a little too hippy-dippy. That's all right. As I've said throughout this book, a lot of this stuff is window dressing. Having said that, I really do believe there is something to be gained from this exercise. If you believe, as I do, that we can accomplish a great deal by learning to work with the energy we have inside ourselves by visualizing it in physical form, the circle-casting exercise is perfect for experiencing this firsthand. Not only does it train the mind by forcing you to hold an image in your thoughts, it helps you understand the power of intention, because the stronger you will your circle to be, the more you will feel its presence around you. I promise.

Once you've cast your circle, sit inside it and continue your meditations. See if you feel different, both physically and emotionally, about performing your work inside the circle you've created than you do when you do it in everyday space. Be aware of any temperature changes you might feel, of any changes in the way you perceive your surroundings, and of any alteration in your responses to things you experience in your meditations.

When you are ready to finish your work for the day, it's important to banish, or open, the circle by sending the energy used to create it back into the world. An excellent way to do this is to imagine the light that has created the circle seeping back into the ground to become once again a part of nature. You could also imagine it flying out into the universe, taking with it your positive intentions as a thank-you. Alternatively, you could imagine drawing it back into your hands, placing your hands on the ground, and sending it back into the earth.

Practice circle casting and banishing for this fourth and final week. At the end of the week, when your term of commitment is about to end, cast your circle, sit inside it, and return once more to the wood of the Horned God. When you meet him, thank him for the time spent with him. See if he leaves you with any parting words or gifts.

When you have left him and returned to the beginning of the path, open your eyes and look over the journal you've been keeping. Look, in particular, at the list you made the first week of things you wanted to accomplish by taking this time to explore the Path of the Green Man. Have you begun to address all (or any) of the things on your list? Was your experience what you had hoped for or thought it would be? How was it different? What was hardest about your time? What was easiest?

Ask yourself all these questions. Most of all, ask yourself if your life has become more fulfilling by walking the Green Man's path. That, after all, is really the point of all of this. If you *have* felt positive changes in your life, ask yourself if Wiccan spirituality is something you want to continue to study. If it is, we'll discuss more in the final chapter about how you begin doing that.

Even if you've decided that your interest in Witchcraft goes no further than this initial period, you've hopefully learned something about yourself and about the ways the Path of the Green Man can be used to express your spiritual journey. Take what you've learned from this and use it in following whatever spiritual path you choose to follow.

RIDING WITH THE WILD HUNT

A Story for Mabon

ABOUT MABON

Mabon is probably the least noticed of the sabbats. Most books on Paganism devote very little space to discussing it, and there isn't very much lore associated with it. This is too bad, as it is a very powerful time of the year.

Obviously, since it is the autumn equinox, Mabon comes on the opposing side of the Wheel of the Year to Ostara, the spring equinox. Where Ostara welcomes the coming of the light and the birth of the sun, Mabon welcomes the coming of the dark and the time when the sun goes to rest.

Welcoming and embracing the changes of the seasons helps us to usher in the new season and see the old one out with our thanks for all it has brought to us. In this story, the Green Man welcomes the arrival of the darkness in his own way. He does so by joining in the Wild Hunt led by Herne the Hunter. Herne is a popular figure in Paganism, representing the wild forces of nature, and especially the forests. He is frequently portrayed as having equal parts of light and dark in him, belonging neither to one side nor the other, which makes him the perfect figure to honor at Mabon.

There is no real basis in any legend for this story. I just liked it. The word *mabon* is Celtic for "young man," which provided the imagery of two boys, one light and one dark. The idea of Herne and the Green Man rounding up the children of light and dark to make them get on with the business of turning the Wheel of the Year appealed to me. In the same way, we can all welcome the coming of the dark with whatever rituals we create.

SUMMER FADED AS the sun crept deeper into the arms of the Earth and darkness tarried longer in the sky each night. The creatures that thrived in the light busied themselves with preparing for the months of cold that were about to visit themselves upon the world, storing up food and building for themselves comfortable homes in the trees of the forests, the banks of the river, and the hidden places of the hills. The fields, shorn of their harvests, lay empty, sleepy, and wide beneath skies that more and more were filled with a dusky twilight.

The Green Man, sensing the changes in the weather, readied himself for the turn of the year as well. He made sure that his cellars were filled with food and his pile of wood replenished with more from the forest. He put warmer blankets on his bed, and more often he found himself wearing his cloak when he went walking after sunset.

The Green Man welcomed the season as he did all the others, with happiness at its arrival and some small sadness at seeing the departure of the preceding one. But there was a special place in his heart for the coming of fall and the darker months. At this time the people of the valley began to close themselves inside, and he felt as if the woods, the fields, and the mountains belonged then to those who chose to venture into the outside and showed more readily the secrets they kept hidden during the warmer months. He knew that there were creatures who preferred the darkness to the light, and he knew, too, that not all of them were as frightening or terrible as the legends would have him believe. Probably, he told himself, they simply wanted to be left in peace to go about their business and think their thoughts.

He loved, too, how the sky was rinsed with purples and grays and how the trees were painted all in oranges, yellows, and reds. The air smelled differently, like cold, smoke, and earth, and the sometimes overwhelmingly sweet perfume of summer flowers aged into a rich scent of pine and earth. Even the night sky seemed clearer and brighter, the stars icy in the velvet blackness that circled the world as he lay in his warm bed and dreamed of all that he would do during the coming season.

Since his supper with Lugh at Lammastide, the Green Man had been busy. He had spent many hours writing down the stories of his life, and he had shared them with all who would listen. Often, he had sat on the hillside until late into the night, sometimes talking and sometimes listening. He had learned much about himself, and about others through this sharing of stories. As he prepared for the season of cold, he was pleased with how far he had come on his journey of the year.

Then came the night when once again light and dark were balanced in the sky. The next time the moon came it would be the dark that was rising and light that was waning, but on this night the two were of equal strength. The Green Man looked at the painted egg sitting on his windowsill and thought once again of Gaia and the day on which he had witnessed the birth of the sun child. He had watched the child grow throughout the summer to his full glory, and he knew that now it was time for him to return to his mother and rest until his rebirth in the spring. He, too, had grown in strength and power during that time and wondered where his path would take him now that his sun companion went elsewhere.

So on the night when light and dark were equal for the second time in the year, he went into the woods to greet the darkness. He knew not how he would find it or in what shape it would come, but he knew that it would be there. As he walked into the shadow of the forest, he felt the cold black night slip around him and he allowed himself to be drawn into its embrace without fear.

He walked for some time without direction, simply picking

his way among the trees and rocks as he felt led. The light from the moon and the stars fell faintly through the branches above, and the forest floor looked in places like a ghostly river rushing over fallen branches and dashing into ferny glens before appearing again on the other side. The Green Man followed the light deeper and deeper into the forest until he passed the towering oak that marked the place that he usually turned back. Going farther, he knew, meant a very long journey home again.

But on this night he strode past the oak, touching it lightly for protection from anything that he might need protection against, and walked farther still into the woods. Here, the branches above were thicker, and the river of light faded to only the occasional patch of misty grayness flickering over a stone or rotting stump. The Green Man could see very little, but still he walked with a sure foot. Around him he heard the calls of the night birds, and they kept him company.

Now, although he did not know it fully, he was in a part of the forest more ancient than all the rest. The trees here had grown to their full height long before the arrival of men in the valley and had seen much. The earth in which their roots entwined was older still, and carried in it the bones of the giants who had first created the hills by digging up the ground in their quest to find the gold that was buried deep beneath it. While the whole of the valley ran with magic, it ran most thickly in the sap of the trees from this place, and the very air was charged with it.

After walking for some time, the Green Man stopped to rest and drink some of the water he had brought with him. He found a tree to rest against and sat in the darkness listening to the forest as it talked to itself. He could understand some of what it said, but much of it was in an old tongue he could not make out.

As he was listening and wondering if perhaps he should turn

back, a figure darted from among the trees and stood near him. It was a boy. His skin was pale as milk, and he wore no clothes. His hair, too, was white, and his eyes shone like silver moons in his face. His bare feet made no sound, but when he saw the Green Man he laughed and it was like the sound of bells.

Before the Green Man could speak, another figure emerged from the trees. This, too, was a boy, naked and identical to the first but colored all in black like the deepest parts of a lake. His eyes were polished stones, and when he saw the Green Man staring at the white boy, he, too, laughed, his voice like rain.

The two boys stood side by side, watching the Green Man. Still, he could not speak, although he tried to ask them who they were and what they were doing in the woods at night and unclothed. But before he could draw breath to do so, there was a great crashing in the woods to his right. The boys looked at one another, laughed again, and ran, the white boy going in one direction and the black boy in another.

A moment later, a great horse charged out of the trees with a rider on his back. It was a man, but a man unlike any the Green Man had ever encountered. He stood twice as tall as any man of the valley. His arms and legs were thickly muscled, and his eyes shone like those of a hawk with a pale golden light. Following him and his horse were a pack of hounds, their fur the color of mist and their eyes glowing red like embers. They moved silently, their noses to the ground and their ears alert as they darted among the trees.

"Merry meet, friend," the man said. "What brings you to my woods on this of all nights?"

The Green Man stood beside the horse and looked up. "I have come to meet the darkness," he said. "I know that tonight it and the light meet for the last time as brothers before the turning of the Wheel."

The man laughed, a great rolling sound that filled the forest.

"Indeed they do," he said. "That is if I can catch them and send them on their way. But at the moment they elude me."

Then the Green Man understood the appearance of the two boys, and what they were about in the woods. "I have seen them," he said. "Not but a few minutes ago."

The man smiled. "So my hounds were indeed on their trail," he said. "Very good. We will have them yet, as we do every year this time. And since you have seen them, perhaps you will be of some assistance. Come, sit behind me."

The man reached down, and the Green Man took hold of his hand. Lifted up, he found himself astride the huge horse.

"It is not every mortal who is allowed to ride with Herne and the Wild Hunt," the man said. "Now hold tightly to me and you will see what it is that happens on this night."

The Green Man gripped Herne's waist tightly as the horse leapt forward with the hounds around it. He felt as if he were flying through the night as the branches swept past him and the Herne led the Hunt deep into the trees. The ghostly figures of the dogs blurred with the shadows as they ran, and their eyes flickered like fires.

They had gone in the direction of the light child, and it was not long before the Green Man saw the boy ahead of them, darting among the trees as he looked behind at the approaching Hunt. He seemed to have no fear, and indeed laughed merrily as they pursued him up one hill and down another, Herne urging his pack forward and the hounds obeying.

Then the boy stumbled leaping over a fallen tree and fell into the soft pine needles on the forest floor. A moment later the hounds had surrounded him, lifting their heads and baying in triumph. Again, the boy showed no fear of them, putting his hands around their necks and allowing them to lick his face. Herne brought the horse to a stop beside them and looked down at the boy.

"A good chase, old one," he said. "But again I and my hounds have triumphed. Now off with you while I attend to your brother. He is younger, and I think perhaps you gave up more easily than you would have us think."

The white child smiled at Herne and stood. With several of the ghostly Hunt in attendance, he walked away into the woods.

"Where does he go?" the Green Man asked.

"To wait for us to finish our business," Herne answered. "You will see."

Again they rode into the trees, this time in search of the child of dark. Being the color of night, he was difficult to see. But as they passed beneath an opening in the trees, the moon shone down and the Green Man saw a shadow slip across the forest floor.

"I see him!" he cried, and the Hunt picked up the scent and began the chase.

As before, they followed on the heels of the boy as he tried to elude them. But again they were victorious as the boy, attempting to hide behind a particularly large tree, gave himself away by laughing as Herne passed by and found himself immediately surrounded by the red-eyed hounds.

"I would like to believe that you did not reveal yourself on purpose," said Herne sternly when he addressed the boy. "However, it is of no matter now that you have been found. Away with you to join your brother. We shall be there shortly."

Again the hounds escorted the boy away into the night. Then Herne turned the horse onto a new path, and they began to walk. The Green Man asked no questions as they went, knowing that he would know soon enough where they went and why.

The horse took them deeper and deeper into the forest, following a path that circled around and around itself, growing ever smaller until they came to the center of the spiral they had been traveling. They passed through a gate of trees and emerged into a clearing. The sky above was filled with stars, but when he looked up at them the constellations they formed were unknown to the Green Man. The circle felt as though it were of a different place from the rest of the forest, as if in traveling the spiral path they had somehow entered a place where time meant nothing.

Herne dismounted and then helped the Green Man off the horse. They stood together by its side and waited. Around the clearing the hounds sat quietly, their red eyes blinking.

"You will now see something older even than these woods," said Herne. "This ritual has been taking place since She made the world and set the Wheel of the Year turning."

Then on either side of the clearing the boys appeared, the white entering from the left and the black from the right. They stood across the empty space from one another and bowed. Then each began walking, the child of light moving to his right and the child of darkness moving to his left. They each circled the clearing repeatedly as they spiraled inward, passing one another at regular intervals but never touching. Finally, they both reached the center, where they stood facing one another.

"Again we meet, brother," said the dark child.

"As we have and always will," said the child of light.

"Tonight you begin your journey back to our Mother and to a much-deserved rest," continued the black boy.

"While you take my place for a time," answered his brother.

The white boy embraced the black boy and kissed him. "Rule well and wisely," he said. "I will return in spring to greet you again."

"And I will wait for you and welcome you," said the dark child. "Go now, and sleep."

The white boy turned and faced away from his brother. As

208 • The Path of the Green Man

the Green Man looked on, the child of light walked out of the clearing and away into the woods, leaving his brother to stand alone.

The dark boy turned to Herne and the Green Man. "You have done well, Hunter," he said. "Your part is finished for another year, at least as far as our business is concerned. You and your Hunt have once again caused dark and light to meet here in this place. Now it is my turn to rule the forest for a season, and I'm sure our paths will cross from time to time."

"I hope that is so," said Herne, bowing his head.

"And you, Green Man, have greeted the darkness well. I thank you," said the child of black. "I trust that in my season you will learn much. Know that I welcome you to my time."

The Green Man bowed also, not knowing what to say. The black boy nodded in return, and then took himself off into the shadows.

"Why did you need to hunt them?" the Green Man asked when he was again alone with Herne.

"They are old, the two," he said. "But still they are children. The child of light does not want to go to sleep, nor does his dark brother want to go to his duties. They must be reminded, and that is my calling. And the calling of all those who honor the turning of the Wheel. You have done so tonight, and so the child of darkness begins his reign. He will walk these woods for many nights now, growing in strength. Soon his laughter will bring the snow, and his songs will cause the winds to blow. But now it is time for you to be away."

Herne helped the Green Man back onto his horse, and they returned through the spiral path with the hounds running all around them on velvet paws. The horse knew its way through the woods, and after some time they came to the great oak that marked the entrance to the Green Man's familiar forest. He dismounted.

"You rode well," said Herne, his golden eyes shining.

"Because I held tightly to you," answered the Green Man.

Herne laughed, and his hounds bayed with him. "Perhaps we will meet again when next I ride," he said. "Until then, listen for the sound of my hounds at night, and know that the child of dark walks the world because you showed the Hunt the way."

Then the Wild Hunt was away after some new quarry, and the Green Man was alone in the forest, surrounded by the first hours of the new season.

Chapter 8

Building a Magical Community

The Path of the Green Man is designed so that it can be practiced by individuals. The Green Man figure in "The Journey of the Green Man" travels the path alone for a reason. Spiritual growth begins with the individual, and for each of us the journey we take is a unique adventure meant to show us what we need to know about ourselves and about our place in the world. Everything in this book can be done on a solitary basis.

At some point, though, you may find that you want to explore your spiritual path with other like-minded people. The Green Men came into being because those of us who were involved in the circle had reached a point in our lives where we felt that working with other gay men would add something to our established practices. Each of us maintained our individual practices and used the group as a way to bring what we had learned—or wished to learn—to the others. By contributing ideas and discussing different issues that came up in our practices, we created something new and different that benefitted from our individual outlooks.

Creating a circle of gay men with whom to explore Green Man spirituality is something you might want to consider at some point. If so, there are a few things you should keep in mind about group work and some basic guidelines for forming and running a circle that will help you create a group that provides an open, positive setting for everyone involved.

Finding Members

The first step in forming a Green Men circle is, obviously, finding other men who are interested in this spiritual path. There are various ways to do this. The original Green Men came together from other groups that were, in some way, connected to either men's spirituality or gay spirituality. Several of us met at a weekend retreat for men focusing on drumming and singing. Others were involved in the Radical Faeries. Some were friends of friends.

If you are already involved in the Pagan or Wiccan community, you will likely know other gay men who share your interests. If so, see if any of them are interested in forming a circle specifically for gay men. Similarly, if you are currently involved in another spiritually oriented group with other gay men, you might see if some of them are interested in exploring Pagan spirituality with you.

Although your immediate group of friends might seem a likely source of participants in a Green Men circle, this isn't always the case. Unless your friends are spiritually inclined to begin with, asking them to explore something like the Path of the Green Man may not be very successful. So, before you invite all the guys over to your house for a Samhain ritual or a Beltane celebration, think carefully about what you know of your friends' attitudes toward spirituality. If they aren't going to take it seriously, forming a study group with them may be more hindrance than help to your own spiritual journey.

Even if you think you don't know of anyone who might be interested in Green Man work, you may be surprised. I've found that once you create the intention to form a community, you find yourself "discovering" interested individuals, often in surprising ways. A chance discussion with someone may unearth a Green Man in waiting. A friend you've never known to have interest in spirituality may suddenly mention a book he's read or something he's seen that has sparked his interest in Wicca. When you decide the time is right to expand your practice into a circle of men, keep yourself open to the possibilities, and you'll find that what you need will come to you.

Remember, too, that a circle can simply be two people. You don't need a lot of men to get started. The idea behind a circle isn't to gather as many people together a possible, it's to create a space in which to share ideas and learn together. Two people can create this kind of space just as easily as six, seven, or twenty can. The important thing is that the men involved share a common goal.

Establishing a Goal

If you've been working with Green Men principles on an individual basis, you've already established a set of goals for yourself. These goals help you keep focused in your spiritual work, and they provide some kind of basis for gauging how you're progressing. This same structure needs to be established for any circle you form with others. You have to have a common goal, otherwise your work together will lack focus and won't benefit anyone fully.

When the Green Men came together, we didn't really have a plan. I'd written the "Green Man Manifesto," which outlined some of the core beliefs we all shared, but other than that we had no set structure as far as how circles would be run or what we would do in these circles. We made things up as we went along.

For the most part, this worked. After a couple of circles, we figured out a basic structure for things and began to discover individual members' talents and utilizing them whenever we could. Men who were particularly adept at designing rituals, for example, were encouraged to use their flare for the dramatic to come up with ideas for celebrations. Those of us who favored writing were often the ones to come up with the different songs or invocations used in the rituals. We had several excellent cooks in the group, who generally provided food for the rituals and after-circle dinners.

In addition to these structural things, we also began to work out the "theology" of Green Men circles. We discussed, for example, whether we wanted to focus on a particular god or use deities from many different spiritual paths. Although we agreed that the Green Man was our obvious choice for a symbol of our group and that the Horned God was our central deity, we needed to determine whether the Horned God would be our exclusive representative of the God or whether we would work with gods from various traditions. Through these discussions, we decided that, to us, the different gods were simply different faces of our Horned God and that working with different ones would allow us to see different aspects of the Horned God's personality. Similarly, we elected to use different goddesses in our rituals as well.

Another thing we discussed as a group was magic, specifically whether or not the Green Men circles would be used to practice magic of various kinds. Again, while we all agreed that simply holding rituals together was a kind of magic, we needed to talk about whether or not we would attempt more overt acts of magic as part of our circles. After much discussion, we decided that, at least at first, our circles would be focused more on ritual and on understanding the essence of Green Man spirituality rather than on working magic.

Why did we make this decision? We felt that it was important for the group to form an identity and for the individual men to come to know one another better before taking our work to another level. We thought that a period of at least one turn of the Wheel of the Year would allow us to do that, after which we could decide how we wanted the group to move forward.

We also established some other guidelines for our circle. For example, we decided that we would not include sexual activity in our rituals. Although sex can be used to enhance magical work, and while some of the sabbats (particularly Beltane) lend themselves to expressing the sexual side of masculinity as embodied in the Horned God, we felt that overtly sexual behavior in the circle would be a distraction from what we wanted to do together. Also, as some of the individual members were using their spiritual studies as a way to deal with the issues of sexual compulsion and addiction, we decided that it was important to create an atmosphere in the group where these men could feel safe to express themselves fully without feeling that they either had to hold back or not participate in certain circles.

These are the kind of things you will need to agree on as a group when you begin working together. People often have different, sometimes completely opposing, ideas of what they want from a circle. By discussing these things before you begin working together, you can establish a basic framework that takes into consideration your different points of view.

Be Flexible

As important as it is to have a basic agreement from which to begin your circle, it's equally important to be flexible. As you continue your work with a circle, getting to know one another and understanding more fully what it is you're all trying to achieve, you'll find that what you do and how you do it changes. As individual men become more comfortable expressing themselves within the group, they may want to contribute new ideas or suggest new ways of doing things. It's important that you create an atmosphere in which these kinds of discussions are possible.

After several rituals with the Green Men, various members began to suggest ideas for rituals that, frankly, I didn't particularly like. My initial reaction was to think, "This isn't what I had in mind when I started this group." The key word here is *I*. I was thinking only about what I thought would make beautiful, interesting, or meaningful rituals. I wasn't taking the time to think that maybe other men had things that were meaningful to them. When I heard their ideas for rituals, I focused on only what I thought was silly about them.

I had to teach myself to let go of my own ideas about what the Green Men "should" be and let myself experience what the other men had in mind. When I did, more often than not I found myself having a much deeper and more enjoyable experience than I had expected to have. I learned that my ideas were not the only valid ones and that by listening to the men I had invited to share my spiritual journey with me, I was taken in new and surprising directions.

Make a Commitment

One of the first things you did as a follower of the Path of the Green Man was to commit yourself to practicing this spiritual path for a certain amount of time. You need to do the same thing with your Green Men circle. Commit yourselves to working together for a set amount of time. And decide how often you will meet (once a week, every full moon, etc.). As I mentioned, the original Green Men elected to work together for one turn of the Wheel, from one Yule to the next. You can do the same thing, or you can choose a shorter amount of time, say from one sabbat to the next.

The important thing is that once you commit to a working period, you stick to it. Although it would be wonderful if every circle that formed worked perfectly and everyone was happy, the reality is that it takes a lot of work. There were many times when I told myself that the Green Men were too much trouble, too much drama, too much time. There were occasional disagreements and even the odd blow-out among members. But we stuck with it because we had agreed to do so, and as a result I think the experience was a positive one for everyone involved.

The more a group works together, the more easily you will find it is to create a magical atmosphere when you come together in your circle. Once you know one another better, slipping into that magical space will start to feel more and more natural. A circle is a partnership, and like any partnership it takes time to establish itself. There will be awkward moments at the beginning, uncomfortable pauses and anxious periods where you're all unsure of yourselves. Work through them. Talk as much as you need to, and remember that you're all there because you're trying to achieve something in and with your lives. If you focus on this common goal, most of the difficulties you encounter can be overcome.

Be sure, too, that you mark the beginning and end of your period of commitment. Do something special to celebrate. And if you decide to continue your circle, make a commitment to another period of time.

Be Patient

It's exciting forming a circle. If you're someone who has been looking for a long time for a spiritual group in which you feel comfortable, bringing together a group of Green Men may seem like a dream come true. And in many ways, it is. But as with the realization of any dream, it's very, very important to remember that nothing is perfect, especially not immediately. You need to have a lot of patience when you form a circle, because I guarantee you that whatever you expect your circle to be, it will be different.

I remember inviting the participants to that first Green Men circle. I was so excited. The men were enthusiastic. I had a great plan for the first ritual. It was all going to be perfect and we would immediately have this amazing group that would become more and more wonderful with every ritual. In my head, I planned out monthly full moon circles, visualized everyone becoming the best of friends, and even allowed myself to think that somewhere down the line we might have, like my Radical Faerie friends, a retreat somewhere in the forest where we could hold large gatherings for men from all over. It was my own little spiritual revolution, and it seemed on the brink of happening.

The reality was not quite as dramatic. The first ritual *was* fantastic. But it soon became clear that, although we shared a common goal, the men in the group all had their own lives apart from the Green Men. Conflicting schedules, partnerships, jobs, and the usual components of everyday life meant that getting the group together on a regular basis was going to be a lot of work. We couldn't all drop everything to dedicate ourselves to forming this community of gay men that was going to take over the world.

At first I was a little disappointed. But when I really sat and thought about it, we had created something even more powerful than what I'd imagined. We had brought together a group of men who, despite everything else going on in their lives, were committed to coming together to explore our common interest in Pagan spirituality. That in itself was a major achievement, and although part of me wanted things to move much more quickly, I came to realize that everything was proceeding exactly as it needed to.

This book is a case in point. From the very first ritual, people suggested that I write a book about Green Man spirituality. But it's taken nearly six years for that to happen. Every so often during those six years I would think about the book and sort of start to work on it, but each time something else came along to push it to the back burner. Then the right time came along and everything fell into place. Now, I see that the book really couldn't have been written until now. There were ideas I needed to clarify and things I needed to experience before I could write the book. Had I rushed it, it would not have been the same book, and ultimately I know it would not have achieved what I wanted it to.

Be gentle with your circle. Treat it like you would a newly sprouted plant or a newborn puppy. Don't place too many expectations on it at first. Let it stumble along, finding its legs and discovering who it is. Let it make mistakes and don't become discouraged when it seems to be something other than what you'd hoped for. This is, in some ways, an experiment, and often we learn more from how experiments don't work out as expected than we do when they come out exactly as planned.

Look Beyond the Circle

Individual practice is the heart of Green Man spirituality, and the circle is an extension of that. But there is a world of other spiritual practices outside the Green Man tradition, and it's important to recognize these traditions, some of which share much in common with the Green Men and some of which are completely different.

If at all possible, I encourage you to explore other traditions and practices, even if it's just reading about them. The principles of Green Man spirituality are a direct result of my personal experiences. Had I not involved myself in different traditions, I might never have come to see why the principles I choose to live my life by are important to me. Had I not participated in other ways of following a spiritual path, I might never have developed the rituals and practices I employ in my life.

Find out what other people are doing, particularly other Pagans and Wiccans. Read books about different types of Wicca. If you can, attend open rituals put on by other groups in your area. Starhawk's Reclaiming Tradition, the Radical Faeries, and other groups frequently hold public gatherings (particularly around the sabbats) and welcome people of all faiths to join them. These are excellent opportunities to see how other people express their spirituality, and if nothing else, you may get some great ideas for your own rituals.

There are also annual events held for Pagans and Wiccans. The Witch Camps run by members of the Reclaiming Tradition (www.reclaiming.org) are enormously popular, as are the Rites of Spring and Twilight Covening celebrations held by the EarthSpirit Community in Massachusetts (www.earthspirit.org). Diana's Grove (www.dianasgrove.com) is a Wiccan retreat, school, and gathering place that hosts numerous events throughout the year, including activities specifically for men. In addition, it runs a year-long "Mystery School" that can be done as a correspondence course for those interested in exploring Wiccan spirituality.

All of these things are ways in which you can explore different avenues of spiritual expression, and of course these aren't the only groups or events that you can participate in; they are simply the ones I myself have participated in and can recommend based on my experiences. It should be noted that these are not necessarily gay events, although gay men are welcome, and I recommend them because I feel that they represent an interesting cross-section of the work being done by Wiccan and Pagan groups.

The Radical Faeries (www.radfae.org) is much more oriented toward gay men, and although far less organized than the other groups mentioned earlier (they thrive on spontaneity and chaos), the Faeries have an extensive worldwide network, including a number of beautiful retreats (called Sanctuaries) where they live out the ideals of Pagan spirituality and community. Faerie energy is wild energy, and their gatherings tend to be artistic, flamboyant, and wonderfully all-inclusive. While they aren't for everyone (as nothing is) they are truly unforgettable experiences, and the Faeries are indeed a major force in gay men's spirituality.

Don't Burn Yourself Out

I have, in my basement, boxes of books about Pagan and Wiccan spirituality. I have, too, boxes of statues, candles, oils, incense, and various tools and paraphernalia associated with Witchcraft. For the most part, I never use them. They're things I acquired when I was caught up in a frenzy of excitement over my spiritual path. I thought that the more magical stuff I bought, the more focused and productive my work would be.

This, of course, wasn't true. I didn't need altar cloths, chalices, and all of the other things I found so enchanting. Sure, they were fun, but in and of themselves they didn't contain any spiritual power. That, I learned quickly, came from within.

It's easy to get caught up in the fun and excitement of Witchcraft. It's fun to buy things that make you feel more magical and that lend an air of witchiness to your home and circles. But it's easy to overdose on this stuff, too. I've seen a number of people become obsessed with being Witches, with looking and acting the part to such a degree that they've forgotten entirely what it was that attracted them to the path in the first place.

Attending rituals, becoming part of the extended Pagan community, and developing your connection with the magical world are all fine and useful things. Becoming more interested in these things than in developing a functional, useable spiritual practice is simply a distraction from the real work of the Path of the Green Man. Don't burn yourself out by becoming what I like to call a professional Pagan. Don't distract yourself from your daily practice with things that, while potentially useful as additions to your journey, are not the journey itself.

You see this kind of burnout a lot in people who enthusiastically embrace any spiritual tradition. They become so caught up in their newfound faith that they spend more time collecting the tools of that faith than they do trying to understand what it's all about and how it really applies to their lives. Sometimes, this is because a person is so excited about having found something that speaks to him that he wants to experience it all at once. More often, though, it's because a person thinks that the

222 • The Path of the Green Man

more he looks and acts the part, the more he really will be whatever it is he's hoping to become.

You don't become a Witch by filling your house with stuff any more than you become a rock star simply by walking around with a guitar or a poet by donning a beret and sitting around in cafés all afternoon. Nor do you become a Green Man by reading every single book on Pagan spirituality and attending every Pagan event you can afford to go to.

Take your time with your spirituality. This isn't a new hobby you're undertaking, it's a lifelong journey. You won't get anywhere any faster by rushing things and throwing yourself headlong into the Pagan world without pausing to reflect on what's happening around you. Go slowly and really take time to examine the different experiences you have and to explore the different directions the path takes you.

This goes for groups as well as for individuals. In fact, groups can have an even more difficult time because the collective energy is so strong. If you find yourself involved with a group of men who want to speed ahead in their magical work because they're so enthusiastic about having found one another, you may need to slow things down a bit.

Talking About Witchcraft with Others

As we discussed very early on in this book, there are numerous misconceptions about what Witches and Pagans are and about what our spirituality entails. If you are open about your spirituality, you can expect to have a lot of discussions with people who want to know more about what it is you are and what it is you do. Be prepared for these discussions and to have people react in different ways to what you discuss with them.

One of the most difficult experiences people who engage in

Wiccan spirituality have is discovering that not everyone in their lives is supportive of their spiritual undertaking. Family, partners, friends, coworkers, and even casual acquaintances often think it's perfectly acceptable to joke about or even openly ridicule Wiccan spirituality. Knowing that this can happen, and preparing yourself to confront such reactions, will help you as you become more open about yourself.

Discussing our spirituality with others is often referred to by Witches as "coming out of the broom closet," a situation most of us can relate to as gay men. Many Pagans and Wiccans are not out about their spirituality precisely because they don't feel like explaining themselves to anyone. And really, a person's spirituality is indeed a private business. We don't generally ask people about their religions because, on some basic level, we know that it's none of our business. For some reason, though, people think Wicca is fair game. Let it be known in some way that you're a practicing Pagan or Witch, and I guarantee you you'll be answering a lot of questions.

For several years I wore around my neck a small pentacle, a five-pointed star representative of the path of Witchcraft. I can't tell you the number of times people asked me what it was and wanted to know why I wore it. Although I often enjoyed the resulting conversations, it frankly became very tiring to always be waiting for the inevitable questions to come at me. Finally, I stopped wearing any outward symbols of the Path, not because I was embarrassed or ashamed of it, but because I just didn't have time to talk about it endlessly.

When I *do* discuss the Path of the Green Man with people, what I tell them is based largely on what I think they will understand. Someone I know well, for example, and who I know is likely to understand what I'm talking about, will receive a fuller explanation of the principles behind the spirituality than will someone I meet casually. People who are obviously approaching the discussion from a negative or hostile standpoint, too, are perhaps treated to a less detailed discussion. I have no interest in converting anyone or convincing anyone that what I believe is right.

Before you "come out" as a Pagan or Witch, know what it is you believe. If you're going to discuss your spirituality, you'd better really understand it yourself, otherwise you're going to look foolish. And remember, no matter how deeply you feel your faith, there are always going to be people who don't get it or who want you to feel that what you believe is ridiculous. This is an opportune time to remember the Law of Three and remind yourself that what other people think about you isn't important.

When working with a circle, it's a good idea to set some guidelines about what, if anything, members will say to other people about their involvement in the group. The privacy of individual members should be taken into consideration, as well as that of the group as a whole. If one person is talking to people in his life about the group, there's a chance that attention will fall on others in the group who might not be as out about their religious practices. Be respectful of one another's stances on discussing group activity.

Similarly, you need to establish a policy about how and when other men will be invited to participate in or join your circle. The original Green Men, for example, found that some of the men in the group wanted to invite friends to join our rituals. Others felt that the presence of men we didn't know would be disruptive to the atmosphere. Therefore, we decided that certain celebrations would be open to guests and others would be closed only to the group. In this way, we were able to welcome men who were interested in learning about the Green Men and could tailor those events to those with little or no experience with Pagan spirituality. The Green Men–only rituals, on the other hand, could perhaps be a little more intensive in the sense that, working only with established members of the group, we could concentrate on our own work.

Make It Fun

This goes along with the "don't burn yourself out" rule. Green Man spirituality is serious business, but your group rituals should also be times of celebration. We always held potluck dinners following our circles, and these quickly became extensions of the work that went on inside the ritual circle. By sharing food and conversation together, we bonded more as a group and came to know one another more deeply outside of our magical work.

Part of the magic of the Green Men for me is the idea of forming community. In that early group we were not just creating a circle of men interested in Pagan spirituality, we were creating a circle of men who would become friends. Our connections to one another extended beyond the Green Men, and we created a network of men who interacted with one another on a number of different levels. Even though I no longer live in the same city as the rest of the original members, I am still in contact with many of them, just as I remain friends with a number of gay men I've met at other Pagan and Witch events.

These days my work is more solitary, but that doesn't mean I am no longer part of this community of gay men who were brought together by our shared interest in Witchcraft. Community is something that exists outside of circles, a bond that connects us to other people even when we don't see them on a regular basis. My magical friends are scattered all over the world.

Some I speak to on a regular basis, while others I am in contact with perhaps only once a year or less. But regardless of how often we talk or see each other, we are part of a community.

So keep it fun. Not every ritual has to be serious, and there's always room for lightheartedness. The Horned God likes a good laugh as much as the rest of us, and Pagan spirituality is all about embracing life to the fullest. Have a good time and be good to one another—your work with whatever group you find yourself a part of will be better for it.

These are simply some basic guidelines I have found helpful in my own work with groups. You will probably come up with many more of your own that you find useful for your particular situation. Remember, there are no hard and fast rules for how we walk the Path of the Green Man apart from those that we've discussed in this book. Green Man spirituality is a living, growing thing, much like the woods of the Horned God. It changes with the seasons, adapting to the needs of those of us who walk the path. By keeping it organic and allowing it to grow as it will, we experience the power of nature, its cycles, and our connection to everything. And that, in the end, is what this is all about.

BABA YAGA TURNS THE WHEEL

A Story for Samhain

ABOUT SAMHAIN

This last of the eight sabbats is probably the one most familiar—at least in its popularized form—to the world. Halloween, with its costumes and candy, its ghoulies and ghosties, is a much-anticipated opportunity for people to flirt with the world beyond the veil.

But Samhain is about much more than just dress-up and chocolate bars. It is the darkest of the sabbats, a time for reflection and for gazing into the future. Its name comes from the Irish Gaelic word for the month of November, and in traditional farming societies it marked the beginning of winter, the time when the last crops were gathered in and the animals slaughtered to provide meat for the coming months of cold. It was, therefore, New Year's Eve, and many Pagans and Witches still celebrate it as such, seeing it as the night when the Wheel makes its final turn into darkness and comes once more to the position from which it began. Many people use this night to communicate with or to remember the souls of those who have died. It is also a night for divination, for looking into the coming year and seeing what path should be taken and what work should be done. With winter coming, it is an excellent time to plan the work for the cold months.

This story closes the story cycle of the Green Man and his journey through the Wheel of the Year. Just as the Horned God initiated him into his journey, now he must be brought to the end of it. I can think of no one better to do that than the ancient grandmother Baba Yaga, the Russian witch mother whose fantastic house awaits us in the darkest woods. She is death, mystery, and teacher all rolled into one. She tells stories and asks questions, and we know that one false move may see us chewed to bits by her sharp teeth. We fear her, but we also know that she is the Great Mother and that she loves us in her peculiar way.

And so it is to Baba Yaga's house that the Green Man goes on this Samhain night. There, he will gaze into the future and see where his path for the next Turning of the Wheel will begin as he draws a card from Baba Yaga's Tarot deck (something you may want to do yourself on Samhain if you enjoy working with Tarot cards). There are many paths to set your foot on as you leave Baba's house—which will you choose?

THE COLD CAME, riding on the wind. It danced across the fields, leaving behind footprints of frost that disappeared with the first warm rays of the sun but tarried longer each morning. It plucked the leaves from the trees and left the branches bare against the sky as they held their hands up and tried to catch the moon, which swelled with pale light as the nights grew darker and longer. The cold knew that its time was at hand, and it laughed a thin laugh and made its bed beneath the stars.

The Green Man was ready for the coming of the cold. He had filled his cellars with food and piled wood outside his door. His gardens sat empty, awaiting their rest, and his tools were cleaned and put away until they would be needed again. His cloak was mended and hung in its familiar place behind the door, and his hat and stick were ready to walk with him whenever he should choose to go outside. Everything was in order.

As the Green Man waited for one season to end and the next to begin, he spent much time thinking about the year that had passed. Seven times the Wheel of the Year had stopped, and seven times he had been shown something of himself and of his world. These things had changed him, he knew. He felt the changes inside his heart, where they continued to work their magic on him as he kept them close and learned their secrets. He had journeyed a great distance, and he knew that this particular journey was soon to end.

But when he thought about what might lie beyond the close of the year, he saw nothing, and this worried him. *Have I come so far, only to lose my way?* he wondered to himself. *Have I learned nothing about who I am and where I am going?* These thoughts troubled him while he was awake, and his dreams, too, were uneasy.

The days shortened and soon the time came when the people of the valley began speaking of spirits and peculiar things seen in the woods. They knew, all of them, that the night would soon arrive when the door between their world and the world they saw only dimly and in visions would open for the length of an evening, allowing passage from one realm to the other. Some told stories of those who had vanished into the other world, either through foolishness or madness. Others talked of creatures who waited for the opening of the door so that they could make their way into the world of men and work mischief of one kind or another. The children listened, wide-eyed, to these stories, while the old ones exchanged knowing looks with one another and recited to themselves the charms to keep their families safe.

The Green Man knew the stories well. When he was a boy, he sat with the others at his grandmother's feet while she stared into the fire and told them about the girl she knew who listened to the sweet lies of a man with eyes like an owl's and followed him through the doorway into a place from which none could rescue her. He knew, too, that the stories were true, and not simply made up to scare the little ones into obedience, as some of the younger people chose to believe. But though he knew these things, he was not frightened by them. He had learned that light and dark were companions, one unable to exist without the other, and both born out of the same joy that created the world.

And so it was that on the night when the door between the worlds opened and the wind from the other side cried in the woods, the Green Man alone of all the valley's people did not lock himself inside. Instead, he took his cloak and his stick and walked toward the sound, hoping it would lead him to his final mystery. He followed it into the forest, where it seemed to rush all about him as it rustled the branches of the trees and attended to its secret business. In the darkness he saw the flicker of eyes and heard the sound of wild laughter. Yet, still he walked on.

As he walked, he found that he was entering a fog that came upon him suddenly. Thin tendrils swirled about his feet and up his legs, and then he was wrapped in soft gray arms. He could still see, dimly, the shapes of the trees, but it was as if a veil had been pulled over his eyes and the images behind it were like the shadows in a pantomime. They seemed to move and change, and sometimes appeared as nothing more than trees and then but a moment later as wild things dancing around him with hands reaching out to touch his face.

He moved forward, trusting his feet to find sure footing, and after a time the fog departed as quickly as it had arrived, as if he had passed through a curtain into another place. The Green Man expected to find himself in a familiar part of the wood, but was surprised to see that what awaited him was a path totally unfamiliar to his eyes. It stretched narrow and rough between the trees, as if seldom walked, and he could see only a short length of it. He turned to see how he had come to be there, but the darkness revealed nothing.

A ghostly light flickered somewhere ahead of him, beyond the point where the path disappeared behind the trees, and the Green Man decided that he would have an easier time moving forward than he would trying to go back through the fog. Setting his foot on the path, he made for the light, hoping that it came from the fire of a friend and not from something that meant him harm. For while he knew that light and dark came from the same source, he knew as well that sometimes one could rise to greater power than the other and that caution was not the same as fear.

Rounding the turn in the path, he discovered the source of the light and stopped. Stuck into the earth beside the path was a stick the height of a man. It had been stripped of its bark, so that it looked like bone, and on its top was a skull, the empty eyes flickering with cold flame. He saw another one some distance beyond the first, and another beyond that one. They led away into the woods, illuminating the path just enough so that anyone walking it would not trip over the roots that crisscrossed it like interlocking fingers.

The Green Man looked at the skull lanterns and at the path they revealed. He knew not where they might lead him, and the sight of them was enough to make him want to go back to his comfortable house. But he knew as well that they led to something he would be able to find only on this night and that if he turned back he would wonder forever after what he might have seen had he kept moving forward. Keeping this thought in his mind, he stepped past the first skull and moved quickly toward the next.

The path led deeper and deeper into the woods, the skull lanterns drawing him into the black night. He could see almost nothing on either side of the path, and the cold light was enough only to see to the next pair of dead eyes. Still the Green Man walked, until finally he came to a clearing in the forest.

In the clearing was a house. It was a very old cottage, the roof covered in moss and the sides overgrown with rose vines thick with thorns and dried blossoms. It was perched precariously atop a gigantic chicken foot, which hopped continually and spun about at a dizzying speed. As the house twirled in the air, threatening at any moment to fly from its peculiar resting place and come crashing down, the Green Man saw that light crackled behind the glass of the windows and smoke trickled from the chimney.

The clearing was circled by a fence made of bones. A gate, its lock composed of jaws and teeth, kept him outside. Yet as he looked at the strange house, the Green Man remembered a story told to him by a very old woman when he was a boy.

Drawing on his scraps of memory, he walked to the gate and said in a strong voice, "Open for me, who has come all this way to see the one whose house this is."

Instantly, the teeth parted and the gate opened. At the same time, the giant chicken foot ceased its mad hopping and crouched low to the ground so that the house seemed to sit on the earth. The Green Man passed through the gate of bones and walked up to the front door, where he knocked firmly three times.

"Who dares bid my house to stop its dancing?" said a voice from within, a voice strong as a killing frost and dark as the winter night.

"I have come to see the owner of this house," said the Green Man.

Laughter spilled from the house then as whomever awaited the Green Man cackled with joy. But it was not a pleasant joy, and the Green Man felt his skin prickle beneath his warm cloak.

"Perhaps you are foolish, and perhaps you are wise," said the voice. "Enter and find out which."

The door to the house opened and the Green Man stepped inside. The door shut behind him, and he stood looking about. The cottage seemed to be much larger inside than it appeared from out, and it was filled with the light of a fire that burned on the hearth. The ceiling was hung with bundles of strange herbs and flowers, and the air was heavy with the smell of roasting meat. At the fire an old woman stood, turning a small pig on a spit and looking at the Green Man with coal black eyes. Her wild gray hair fell nearly to her feet, and her clothes were the color of earth.

"Thank you for your hospitality," said the Green Man.

The old woman opened her mouth, showing a tangle of teeth sharp as knives. "I have given you nothing yet," she said. "And what I do you may not be so thankful for. Why have you come to my house on this of all nights?"

"I think, Baba Yaga, that it is only on this night that I could have come here," answered the Green Man.

The old woman grunted. "So, you know my name," she said. "I suppose you think yourself a clever man."

The Green Man shook his head. "Not clever," he said. "I have simply heard your name spoken and remembered it."

"Nonetheless, it has saved you," she said. "This time. For if you knew not where or to whom you had come, I would have eaten you in a thrice. But since you do know, you may stay as a reward for listening well to the tales some tell about me."

Baba Yaga mumbled something the Green Man could not hear, and immediately three pairs of hands appeared in the air around her. They busied themselves laying a table and taking the roasted pig from the spit. They gathered bread, butter, and jugs of beer and brought them to where Baba sat waiting. When the food was set before her, she ate ravenously, her hands pulling meat from the bone and ripping the bread into chunks that filled her mouth.

The Green Man watched as Baba Yaga ate, saying nothing. When she was done, she pushed her empty bowl away, drained her mug, and looked at him. She cocked her head to one side and fixed him with a dark eye.

"You say nothing," she said. "Do I frighten you?"

The Green Man looked at the ancient figure before him. She was older than the woods, older than the moon, and older even than time.

"You frighten me as death frightens me," he said. "I know that it will come, yet I do not know enough to meet it with open arms."

Baba Yaga laughed again. "They all fear death," she said, speaking to herself. "Yet death is only the beginning of life."

She looked back up at the Green Man. "Very well," she said.

"Since you have come, you will receive what you seek. But only after you answer me three questions."

"And if I fail?" asked the Green Man.

Baba Yaga smiled her terrible smile. "Then perhaps you will meet death sooner than you might otherwise," she said. "The way to my house is lit with the skulls of those who could not answer me."

The Green Man thought about the empty eyes of the skulls. Then he drew up a chair and sat at the side of the table opposite Baba Yaga. The three pairs of hands appeared and whisked away the remnants of her supper and swept the crumbs into the fire. When it was bare, Baba Yaga sat back in her chair and looked at the Green Man.

"What is your greatest gift?" she asked.

The Green Man thought about the year through which he had walked. He had received many gifts from those he met along the way, and discovered even more gifts within himself. Each one seemed more special than the last, and he found it hard to choose from among them. Brigid's words of power had filled him with warmth, and the kiss of Pan had awakened his desires. Maeve had made him a king, and Lugh had shared his friendship. The Green Man himself had shared his songs and his stories. He had helped birth the Child of Light, and had joined Herne on the Wild Hunt. All of these things were worthy, but he knew that they were not enough for Baba Yaga. And then, as he thought about his journey, an answer came to him.

"Faith," he said, and knew that it was true. "Not blind devotion, but knowing that going forward along the path will bring me new knowledge and new challenges. It is what allowed me to dive from the Horned God's high cliff and begin my journey, and it is what brought me here tonight although I might have turned back."

Baba Yaga nodded her head. "Very well," she said. "I see

that our lessons have not been entirely wasted on you. And now answer me this: What is your greatest fear?"

The Green Man opened his mouth to say that death was his greatest fear. He had said almost as much to Baba when she asked if he was frightened of her, and it seemed to him that it was what all men truly feared in their hearts, no matter how brave they may be. But just as he was about to say it, he found that it wasn't true at all. There was something he feared far more. "I fear no longer wanting to know what lies ahead of me," he said. "I fear reaching a place where I foolishly believe that I have learned all there is to learn, for that will mean that the path has become too difficult for me."

Again Baba Yaga nodded. "You were not entirely truthful when you told me that you were not clever," she said. "But we shall see how clever you are when you answer me this last question. Tell me, what can you give Baba Yaga that she does not already have?"

This question puzzled the Green Man. Baba Yaga was the Mother of Time. She had in her possession all that she could possibly want, and what she didn't have she could take without asking. Nothing was forbidden to her. She held life and death in her gnarled hands and played with them as a child might play with a ball. What could he have that she did not?

Baba Yaga watched the Green Man with stony eyes. She did not move at all as he thought long about her question. She was as still as a mountain and as quiet as snow, until he thought that perhaps she had gone to sleep.

"Well?" she asked, breaking the silence. "The night grows old with my waiting."

The Green Man closed his eyes and let his mind clear. Images came to him from his travels: the fires on the hillside at Imbolc, the horses in the field carrying John Barleycorn to his death, the sounds of lovemaking in the fields on Beltane night.

Each one reminded him of a place, or a person, he had loved with all his heart. And that was when he knew what only he could give.

"My love," he said. "It is the only thing that is truly mine and mine alone. My songs and my stories are reflections of the world. My carvings, the food that I cook, my garden—all are created out of things that are not really mine alone. But my love comes only from me. No one can take it from me by force, and when I give it I give it freely, even when I give it foolishly and it is not returned. That is the only thing I can give to you that you cannot take for yourself."

Baba Yaga's eyes reflected the dancing flames of the fire as she looked long at the Green Man. He looked into those eyes, and he saw that he was right.

"And do you give it?" she asked.

The Green Man looked at the terrible face of Baba Yaga. She was old, and some thought wicked. She could be hard, cruel, and demanding. Yet, he loved her. He loved her because she asked him to see what was true, and to look at the darkest part of himself and return stronger and more determined than ever to walk the path on which he had set foot. She was the mirror of the world, the mirror of his soul, and she showed nothing but what was already in his own heart.

"Yes," he said. "I give it to you, and gladly."

"You have answered me truthfully," she said. "And now I will give you a gift in return."

A pair of hands appeared above the table and set in front of Baba Yaga a pack of cards. She took them in her hands and shuffled them slowly, letting them fall between her fingers like leaves. After a time, she spread them out before the Green Man.

"Each card represents a different path," she said. "The path you have walked this year ended tonight at this house. Now it is time to set out on your next journey. My gift to you is that you will be allowed to select for yourself the path you will travel in the coming year. It is a precious gift, and even if you should draw a path that is hard, it will be one of your own choosing."

The Green Man looked at the cards lying on the table. His heart trembled as he thought about all the possible paths whose faces were invisible to him. Some, he knew, were harder than others. Some might even bring moments of great difficulty. He could choose only one, and for a moment he feared picking one that would be too demanding. But then he recalled the path he had just walked, and he knew that whatever card awaited him, it would bring him riches beyond his imaginings. And knowing that, he reached out and chose a card.

He turned it over and looked at its face. Baba, too, looked at his choice. Her eyes sparkled and her mouth opened in a sharp-toothed smile.

"So it will be," she said. "And now we must fly. The night nears its ending, and it is time for you to be on your way."

The Green Man placed the card he had selected in his pocket. Then he followed Baba Yaga as she stood and walked to the door, throwing it open. In the yard, he saw her mortar and pestle waiting. Baba Yaga climbed into it and motioned for the Green Man to follow.

"I said that you would receive only one gift tonight," she said as the mortar rose into the air. "But you shall receive two. You shall ride with Baba Yaga on this night as we welcome the new year."

Using her pestle to row through the night sky, Baba Yaga guided the mortar above the forest. All about them flew the spirits who came out to dance in the new year. Baba Yaga called them by name as she sailed through the sky, laughing her fierce laugh and snatching at the stars and gobbling them down when they got in her way.

Again, they passed into a thick fog, and as they did so the Green Man felt the mortar tip. He fell out into the night, and as he tumbled down he heard Baba Yaga cackling high above him. Then he knew no more.

When he awoke, he was in his own bed. The fire had burned down to glowing embers, and outside his window the sky was streaked with gray as dawn began to rise from sleep. He rubbed his eyes and stretched his arms, thinking about his visit to Baba Yaga's house. He reached into his pocket and found there the card he had drawn from her pack. He looked at it again, at the picture that represented his next journey, and he knew that much awaited him. Dressing quickly, he went to the door of his house, opened it, and greeted the new year with all the joy in his heart.

Endings

If you have read this book all the way through, you have traveled with the Green Man on his journey through one turn of the Wheel of the Year. Like him, you now stand at the beginning of your own path, ready to set out on what will be an incredible adventure in the lands of the Horned God.

If you haven't yet begun your period of committed study, begin it now. If you've already completed your initial time of commitment to practicing Green Man spirituality, don't stop here. There will, I hope, be additional books about taking Green Man spirituality further. But you have the tools you need to continue your journey already. Continue to explore the path by reading, practicing, and learning as much as you can about Paganism, Witchcraft, and how these spiritual traditions apply to your life. Celebrate the sabbats and continue to establish a relationship with the Green Man and the Horned God. Explore your connections to the world and particularly to other people. The principles of Green Man Wicca come alive only when practiced, so use them to make changes in your life.

At some point you will ask yourself, "Is this really working for me?" To answer that, ask yourself the following questions:

Do I feel more positive about myself?
Do I feel more positive about the direction my life is taking?
Do I feel good about changes I'm making in my life?
Do I feel as if I'm starting to become the man I want to be?

If you can answer yes to these questions, then you're on the right path. The ultimate goal of Green Man spirituality—as it should be for any spirituality—is to effect positive changes in our lives that help us to become the people we want to be, which will then help us to make a difference in the world at large. Everything about Green Man Wicca is centered around strengthening our ability to create change, starting from within. The rituals, meditations, and magical exercises all teach us how to focus our thoughts and energies on creating these changes.

If you truly practice the Path of the Green Man, you will experience changes in your life. Some will be small, barely imperceptible at first, while others will be more dramatic. Whether you walk this path alone or in the company of other Green Men, you will find yourself learning more about yourself and about your place in the world than you ever imagined. Your journey will not always be easy, but it will always be filled with challenges and surprises. By walking the Path of the Green Man you are committing yourself to exploring your connection to the world and everything in it. Each step you take will lead you deeper into the world of the Horned God and closer to what you hope to find there.

This path has no true ending. Like everything in nature, it is a cycle, one that will bring you time and again to a new place of beginning, to new adventures and new journeys. This book is just the starting point for your initial journey. I hope it leads you somewhere new and exciting and that wherever it takes you, you find something there that enchants you.

Suggested
Readings

Adler, Margot. *Drawing Down the Moon: Witches, Druids, Goddess-Worshippers and Other Pagans in America Today*

Published in 1979, this classic by the National Public Radio columnist, Adler introduced many Americans to Witchcraft for the first time. Along with Starhawk's *The Spiral Dance*, it is probably most responsible for the growth of interest in Witchcraft in America during the 1980s.

Briggs, Robin. *Witches and Neighbors*

An academic account of the Witchcraft persecutions in Europe. I like the thorough research done by Briggs, and I think his evaluation of the reasons for what we call the Burning Times are good. It is also refreshing to see the myths surrounding this period dispelled. However, I find his sometimes patronizing attitude to be off-putting. Still, this is an excellent look at the psychological and social causes of the persecutions, and the tone should not prevent you from getting a lot from the book.

Conner, Randy P. *Blossom of Bone: Reclaiming the Connections Between Homoeroticism and the Sacred*

Conner's now out-of-print book, published in 1993, was one of the first to examine the role of homosexuals and sexually ambiguous people in spiritual traditions. While not specifically about Witchcraft, it is nevertheless an interesting examination of one aspect of gay spirituality.

Crowley, Vivianne. *Wicca: The Old Religion in the New Millennium*

While not everything in here is as I would do it, everything in here is useful. More than that, it is all serious, with none of the woo-woo stuff that sometimes bothers me about Wiccan books. Crowley covers many aspects of the Craft that others don't, and she does it in a practical, thoughtful way. I especially like her discussions of initiation and the fundamental aims of Witchcraft.

Cunningham, Scott. *Wicca for the Solitary Practitioner* and *Living Wicca: A Further Guide for the Solitary Practitioner*

Cunningham, a gay man, took a lot of heat from some parts of the Wiccan community for his two books devoted to Witches who practice solo. Both books are good primers on beginning a personal practice, and Cunningham really opens Wicca up to those who might be afraid to attempt practice out of concern for doing everything the "correct" way.

Evans, Arthur. *Witchcraft and the Gay Counterculture*

Arising from the fervor of the gay rights movement, this book, published in 1977 and now out of print, is interesting as being the first of its kind to link the struggle for gay rights with the persecution of Witches in history. I don't buy the connection completely, nor do I support his suggestions that achieving equality by any means necessary is acceptable, but Evans makes some interesting points, and as an artifact of gay spirituality, this is a valuable read.

Gardner, Gerald B. *Witchcraft Today* and *The Meaning of Witchcraft*

Witchcraft Today was the first book about Witchcraft written by an out Witch, which given its year of publication (1954) was a very big deal. Both books (available in reprint editions) are very dry and often get way too much into theoretical possibilities about the origins of the Craft, but they're fascinating for their place in Wiccan history and for the way they show how people thought of Witches and Witchcraft in the 1950s.

Hill, Frances. *A Delusion of Satan: The Full Story of the Salem Witch Trials*

A truly remarkable day-by-day look at the events surrounding this tragic period in American history.

Hutton, Ronald. *The Triumph of the Moon: A History of Modern Pagan Witchcraft*

Absolutely *the* best book (in my opinion) about the origins of modern Wicca. Hutton's scholarship is first rate, and he debunks a lot of the myths that get passed around by Witches and non-Witches alike about where Wicca came from.

Penczak, Christopher. *Gay Witchcraft: Empowering the Tribe*

The first book to really examine Wicca in the lives of gay men, this book doesn't provide a framework for a new tradition so much as it acts as a Wicca 101 class, complete with suggestions for rituals and spells.

Starhawk. *The Spiral Dance: A Rebirth of the Ancient Religion of the Goddess*

The book that started it all for many a modern-day Witch. Although some of the claims made in the book regarding the origins of the Goddess tradition have been largely disproved, this is still a sound introduction to the whys and hows of female-centered spirituality.